Dear Kumiko, Dear John

Colin New

Japan Library Ltd
Sandgate, Folkestone, Kent

Japan Library Ltd
Knoll House, 35 The Crescent
Sandgate, Folkestone, Kent, England CT20 3EE

First published by Japan Library 1991

ISBN 0-904404-77-3

The publishers wish to express their sincere thanks to The Japan Foundation
for their kind assistance and support in the making of this book.

British Library Cataloguing in Publication Data

**A CIP catalogue record for this book
is available from the British Library**

Set in Souvenir Light 12 on 13½ point
by Visual Typesetting, Harrow, Middlesex
Printed in England by BPCC Wheatons Ltd., Exeter

Contents

Acknowledgements

I would like to thank the following people for their help in the preparation of this book:
My teaching colleagues, but especially
Susan Allen, Howard Bates, Hilary Camm, Pamela Gledhill and
Paul Hopkinson;

The children of Hatfield First and Middle and Gleadless Nursery
First and Middle Schools, Sheffield;

Mavis Pilbeam
(formerly Education Officer, Japan Information & Cultural Centre,
Embassy of Japan)

and
Marion New

ILLUSTRATIONS

Every effort has been made to contact the copyright holders of the illustrations published in this book; where it has not been possible to do so, the publishers apologise for any inconvenience caused.

All Nippon Airways (ANA) 106; AMOS 22; Derek HOLLAND 10; Fuji Press 20; John GREENLEES 25, 26, 28, 48, 50, 51, 52, 75, 80, 95, 99, 100, 104, 105, 121; International Society for Educational Information 18, 54, 59, 68, 71, 76, 103; Japan Airlines (JAL) 106; Japan Library 8, 34, 56, 67, 78, 81, 82, 83, 100, 102, 108, 109, 110, 112, 119, 130; JNTO 111; Japan Times 63; Sam JONES 78; Kabukiza 60; Gordon LOBBAN 11; Fosco MARAINI 77; Colin NEW 24, 73, 100, 116; National Film Archive 57; Hideyuki OKA 116; Ian READER 87; Urasenke Foundation 13, 56; Tim WARD 14, 15; Chris WILLIAMS 10, 30; Catrin WOODEND 14, 15.

Drawings by Irene Sanderson

Long Vowels

As you are reading this book you will see that some of the letters 'o' and 'u' have little lines over them, e.g. Tōkyō and Kyūshū. The lines show you that these vowels are long vowels and have to be pronounced in a special way when you say them if you want to sound really Japanese. The long ō sounds like 'aw' in paw (Tawkyaw); the long ū sounds like 'oo' in boot (Kyooshoo).

In Japan, if you mixed up your long and short vowels people would not be able to understand you. The meaning might even change completely. The little lines are called macrons. We have used macrons all through the book to remind you how Japanese people pronounce their place-names and other words.

Brainstorm Japan

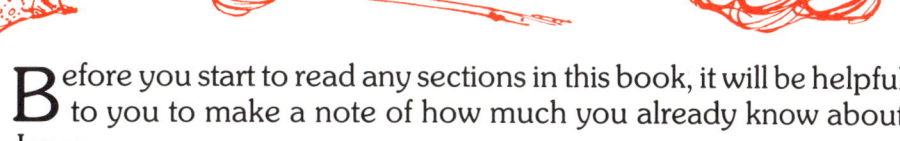

Before you start to read any sections in this book, it will be helpful to you to make a note of how much you already know about Japan.

Split yourselves up into groups of about 5 or 6. Take a large sheet of paper and a felt tip pen. Elect one person in your group to be the scribe. It needs to be someone who can write quickly. Now in your groups take 10 minutes and write down all you can about Japan.

Do not spend time discussing or questioning if you are correct. Just write down whatever the members of your group say about Japan.

Think about the questions below. Your group will probably have a number of answers to each question. They may disagree with each other.

(1) What do Japanese people look like?
(2) What do they eat in Japan?
(3) What clothes do they wear?
(4) What sort of houses do they live in?
(5) What are Japanese people like?
(6) What Japanese words do you know? Yes you do - how about Hitachi, Suzuki and Toyota?

Write down anything else you know about Japan and the Japanese.

When all the groups have finished get together and have a short discussion with your teacher. Do not spend too long on this. Now carefully pack these sheets away. They will be needed again at the end of your project.

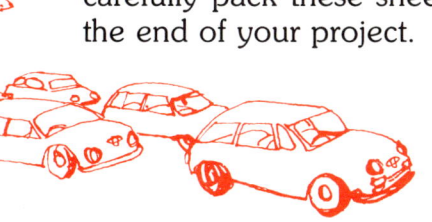

A Note For Students

Project books.

This book will help you to plan your own project about Japan and the Japanese way of life. If you use it properly, it will also help you to think about yourself and your own way of life.

As you use the book, you will see that there are questions to think and write about. These will help you to make your project book. You will not be expected to answer all the questions - indeed to answer some of them will probably take you quite a long time. It is far better to choose one or two questions and answer them really well than to rush and try to answer every question in the book without thinking. Your teacher will help you get a good balance of questions to answer.

You might find the 'To Copy in your Project Book' section of questions a starting point for your work. However, do remember that the other questions are the important ones and they will take a good deal longer to answer. They will also need a lot of thinking about.

There are also some things to discuss and talk about with your friends or teachers. Almost certainly you will find that you do not always agree with each other. Do not be tempted to think that because you are talking that it is not as important as writing things down. Also, try to remember that if you want people to listen to you and your ideas, you must also develop the skills of being a good listener. Your teacher will help you to organise this part of your project.

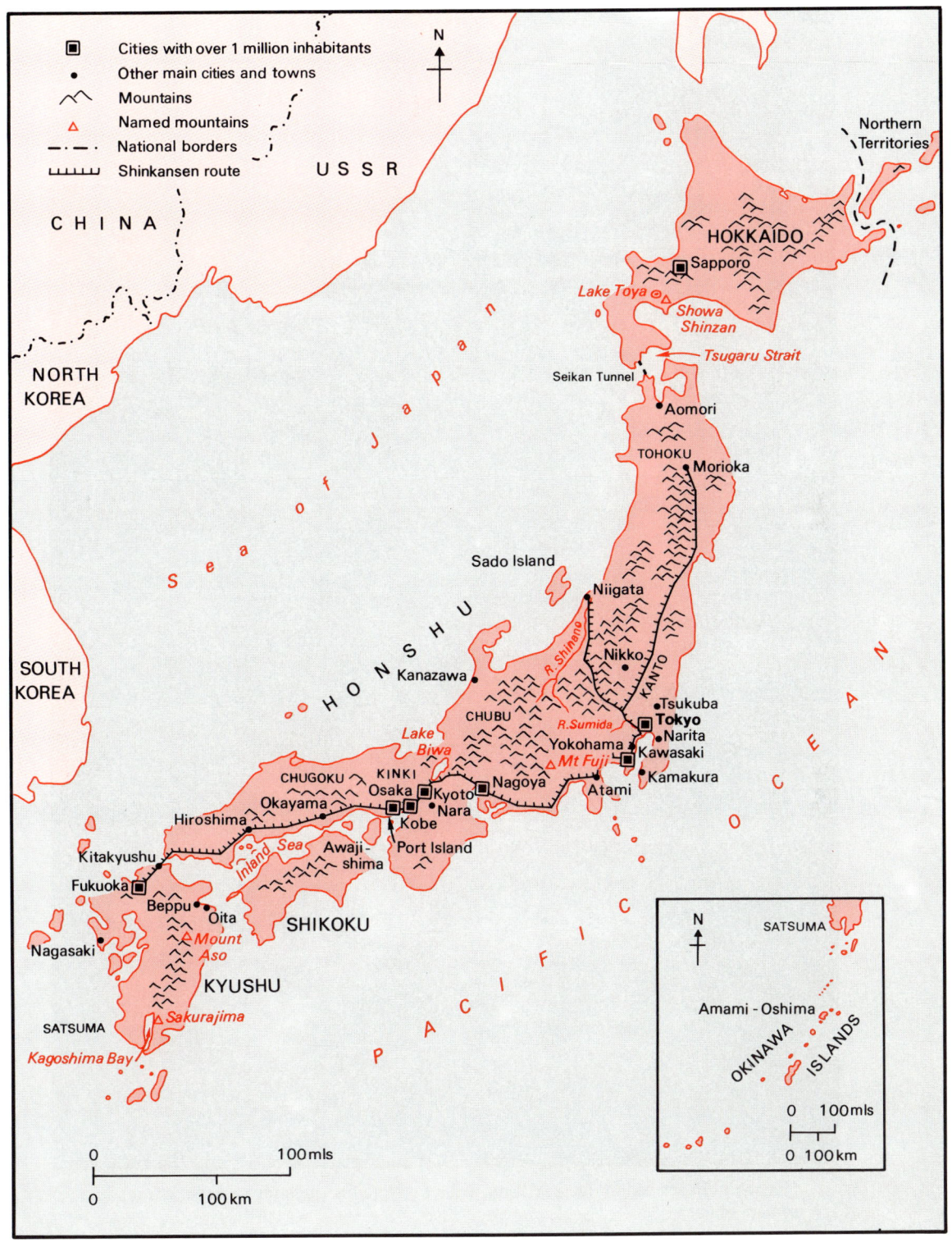

Cities with over 1 million inhabitants
Other main cities and towns
Mountains
Named mountains
National borders
Shinkansen route

N

CHINA

USSR

Northern
Territories

HOKKAIDO

Sapporo

Lake Toya

Showa
Shinzan

Tsugaru Strait

Seikan Tunnel

NORTH
KOREA

Aomori

TOHOKU

Morioka

Sea of Japan

Sado Island

Niigata

HONSHU

R. Shinano

Nikko

KANTO

SOUTH
KOREA

Kanazawa

Tsukuba

CHUBU

R. Sumida

Tokyo
Narita

Lake
Biwa

Nagoya

Yokohama
Kawasaki

Mt Fuji

CHUGOKU

KINKI

Kamakura

Okayama

Osaka
Kyoto
Nara

Atami

Hiroshima

Kobe

Awaji-
shima

Port Island

Inland Sea

Kitakyushu

Fukuoka

Beppu

Oita

SHIKOKU

Nagasaki

Mount
Aso

PACIFIC OCEAN

SATSUMA

KYUSHU

Sakurajima

Kagoshima Bay

N

SATSUMA

Amami - Oshima

OKINAWA   ISLANDS

0   100mls

0   100 km

0   100mls

0   100 km

Hiroshima Peace Memorial to Young Victims. (Note the garlands of paper cranes as a symbol of life.)

Letter 1

Minami Junior High School,
Hiroshima City,
Hiroshima Prefecture,
Japan.

July 15th

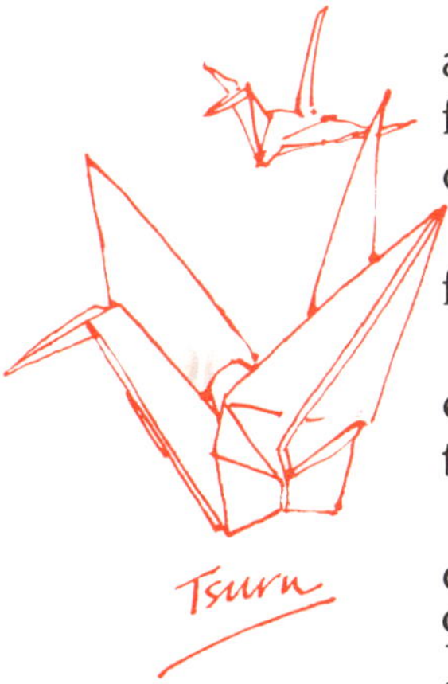

Dear Friends,

How do you do? We are the members of the English Club and we are very glad to write to your school. Here is a box of folding paper cranes, which is a symbol of Hiroshima, a symbol of peace.

Our school is located in the suburbs of Hiroshima City facing the Inland Sea.

Our school opened last year, so we don't have enough equipment for the school, but we are studying many things and training ourselves through sports.

In our school there are about 710 students and 17 classrooms. There are about 40 students in each class. We study 9 subjects and also moral education (citizenship). After school we do some club activities. Each student belongs to his club and enjoys it.

The school year begins in April. Summer vacation is from the 20th of July to the end of August. We have our Athletics meeting in September.

In November we will have the school festival. We are going to do the play 'The Merchant of Venice' by Shakespeare in English.

How is your school?
What do you do in school?
Where is your school?
If you answer us, we will be very glad.

Your friends,
The English Club,
Minami Junior High School,
Hiroshima City,
Hiroshima Prefecture,
Japan.

Tsuru

TO TALK ABOUT

If you received a letter like this at school, how do you think you would reply? What sort of letter would you want to send? If you were Japanese do you think you would sooner receive one letter to the whole club, or a personal letter just to you?

TO FIND OUT AND MAKE

In the letter what is meant by 'folding paper cranes.' See if you can get a book about 'Origami' or 'Paper Folding.' Try to make some of the paper models.

TO WRITE ABOUT

Write a reply to a penfriend in Japan answering their questions about your school. Do you perform plays? Are you a member of a club? The Hiroshima children sent folded paper birds - called cranes - as a symbol of their city. Can you think of something to send with your letter that would be a good symbol of the place where you live?

In your letter try to tell your penfriend something about yourself and your way of life. Do you have a nickname? What jobs do you do about the house? Which foods do you enjoy? What sort of clothes do you like wearing most? Do you have a favourite pop group? Try to make your letter as interesting as possible.

Since you do not know your penfriend's name start your letter 'Dear Friend.....'

Left: Calligraphy lesson in a Junior High School. *Above:* Junior High School in Mie Prefecture.

FOCUS 1 **Home**

'Too Far, Too Small, Too Much!'

'Home is where my family live, but not where I take my friends!'

Japan is a very mountainous country and also it has a large population, so the demand for land for housing is so great that there is hardly enough to go round. Therefore, Japanese town and city dwellers tend to live much closer together than we do. Also the cost of land, especially in the big cities, is very high. Many Japanese homes are much smaller than ours and families have never had much privacy - perhaps this is why they seem to get on well together in groups. If you are living in a small flat or apartment, there is simply no room for selfish behaviour, such as turning up your hi-fi very loud. Parents and children, and sometimes grandparents, too, have to be aware of the needs of others. This does not mean to say that all Japanese children are well-behaved all the time. It is also important that the limited space available is wisely used.

Hiroshima City today.

Heavenly Style

Ikebana

In our country, it is usual for us to invite our friends home. In Japan this is not quite so common. Japanese children might go round to play at each other's houses, but after lessons they also spend much time together at school in club activities, sports practices or having extra lessons. Parents are rarely invited out as a couple. The father's free time is often spent with friends from work, and the mother joins local clubs such as the housewives' chorus-group or does *ikebana* (flower-arranging) with her neighbours. Because couples do not go out together very much, there is not so much need for baby-sitting in the evenings. Japanese people do not often entertain strangers, especially foreigners, at home - it is thought to be easier and more thoughtful to do this elsewhere.

If, however, you were lucky enough to be invited to a Japanese home you would notice many differences. The kitchen might take a much smaller share of the space than is customary in our homes, though kitchen-diners are now very common in Japan. The bathroom would certainly be very different, as we shall see later.

It is almost impossible to say what a typical Japanese home is like these days. But then, what is a typical home here in your own country? Is it a suburban house, or a semi-detached council (municipal) house, or a high-rise flat, or a new modern bungalow or town house? In Japan there are also many variations - modern detached houses, often with one or two traditional rooms, very small compact flats, or, in the countryside, there are still some of the large old-style farmhouses.

The Traditional Japanese House

The traditional Japanese house is a wooden building with lath and plaster walls. This style of building has been used for hundreds of years. The original designers seemed to be thinking more about Japan's hot summers than the cold winters, for while these houses are wonderfully cool and airy in summer, they can be bitterly cold and draughty in the winter months, especially in the snowy north of the country. The designers also had to make use of building materials that were easy to obtain. For this reason wood was used rather than stone or brick. Many of these houses may not look particularly attractive from the outside - their chief beauty is inside, in the sensitive way that natural materials, mainly wood and paper, are used. The colours are quiet and restful.

Traditional houses are divided up into different rooms by sliding

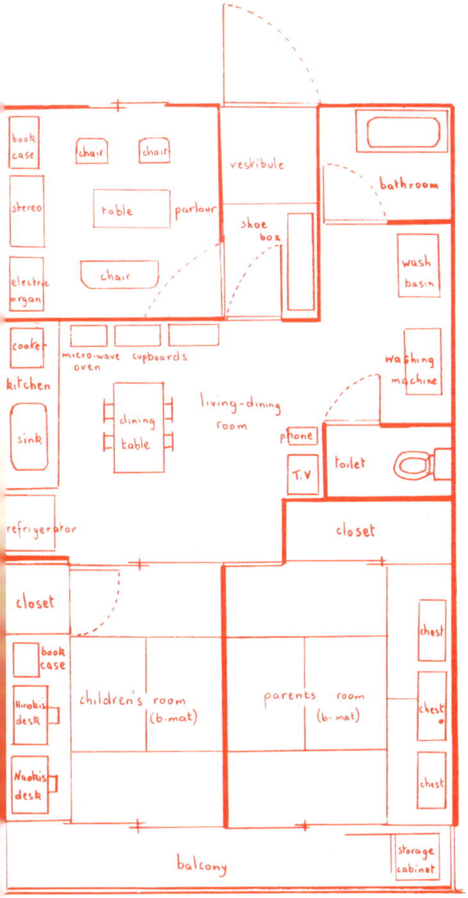

Plan of a typical Japanese house (floor plan with labels):

book case · chair · chair · vestibule · bathroom · stereo · table · parlour · shoe box · wash basin · electric organ · chair · cooker · kitchen · micro-wave oven · cupboards · washing machine · sink · dining table · living-dining room · phone · toilet · T.V · refrigerator · closet · closet · book case · Hirohis desk · Naohis desk · children's room (6-mat) · parents room (6-mat) · chest · chest · chest · balcony · storage cabinet

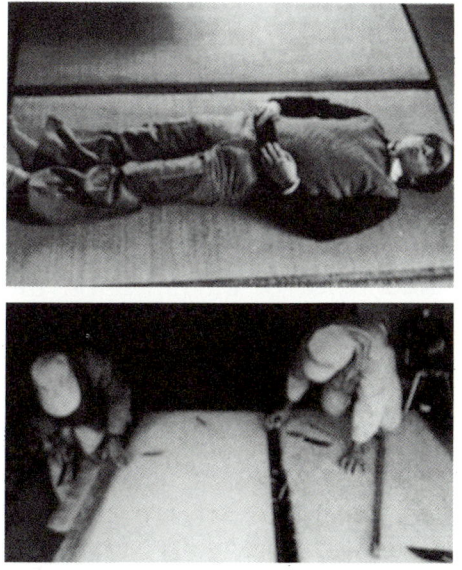

Clockwise: Plan of a typical Japanese house: two pictures showing traditional Japanese room (note the *fusuma* and *tatami*); *tatami* mat-makers; a *tatami* mat is meant to be big enough to fit a man lying down.

Above: A traditional Japanese house in the countryside. *Top left:* A modern home.

partitions. There are two types of partition - *shōji*, which act as doors and windows (they are covered in thin cream-coloured paper which lets the light filter into the room), and *fusuma* which are often decorated, perhaps with a simple flower pattern. *Fusuma* are more substantial - a sort of sliding thick paper wall. Most of the floor-space is covered with straw matting called *tatami*. *Tatami* are usually 1.8 metres long and 0.9 metres wide. They are about 8 cm. thick and are made of rice straw covered with a fine layer of rush.

 Tatami are kept very clean. Their standard size has led to the custom of referring to the size of rooms by the number of mats in them, such as 'six-mat' or 'eight-mat' rooms. The mats fit so closely together that they are rather like enormous straw tiles. *Tatami* have probably had a lot of influence on the way the Japanese live at home. Shoes are left in the entrance-hall to protect the *tatami* from dirt and wear. There is very little heavy furniture because heavy weights cut into the straw. *Tatami* also provide a mattress-like surface to the floor, comfortable and springy to walk on, and so making the change of use from living-room to bedroom easier.

 The big advantage of the traditional room is that it can be both bedroom and living-room. At bed-time the door of the fitted

Sewing tatami

cupboard is slid open and the bedding (*futon*) that has been neatly stored during the day is taken out. A thin mattress (*shikibuton*) is laid on the *tatami* and a quilt (*kakebuton*) inside a cotton cover is put on top. It is rather like a continental duvet. Pillows are small, fat and rather hard. In the morning the bedclothes are put out to air and then folded neatly back into the cupboard. The low table and cushions are replaced in the centre of the room and the change from bedroom to living-room is complete.

Modern Apartments

New apartment buildings

Skyscrapers in Japan have become common for office and hotel accommodation since the invention of new earthquake-proof building techniques. One of the tallest skyscrapers in Tōkyō is the 60-storey Sunshine Building, but tower-block housing is not a common feature of Japan in the way it is in our cities. Blocks of flats are usually no more than ten storeys high. The residents will often have an active residents' group which organises various committees such as the garden committee which cares for the environment of the flats.

More and more city-dwellers are now living in modern flats. Often these have central heating, wall-to-wall carpeting, a main room with western-style tables and chairs, lounge suite, hi-fi, video and television set. The living space in these flats is usually very cramped. By dividing the rooms with solid walls rather than sliding screens, the designers have given up traditional flexibility for modern living styles and warmth. It is easier to keep several little rooms warm than it is to heat up one very large room subdivided by paper screens.

Left: Traditional wooden houses in the city. *Right:* Modern apartment blocks (*danchi*) near Tokyo Bay.

Tokyo: the new 'skyscaper' centre of Tokyo dwarfs the traditional one- and two-storey buildings of the residential areas.

Public opinion surveys show that, ideally, most Japanese people would like to own a two-storey house with enough room to mix modern western comforts with the traditional Japanese life-style. Many people now choose to use chairs (they use them all day at school and at work), although they still like to use a low table and floor cushions on special occasions. Some people prefer sleeping on interior-sprung mattresses on western-style beds, and children often have bunk-beds. Most families have started to collect belongings for which the traditional home does not have space. For example, more people own a colour television set (99%) in Japan than any other country in the world. The percentage of Japanese who own the following items is also very high: cameras (85%), stereos (59%), pianos (20%), air-conditioners (59%), video-cassette recorders (53%), washing-machines (99%), micro-ovens (57%), refrigerators (98%) and vacuum-cleaners (98%). On average every household takes two daily newspapers, and more books are purchased in Japan than in any other country. Possessions, like people, need their own space in a home.

Perhaps it is not surprising that while 60% of Japanese people own their own houses many of them still complain about not having enough space. In Tōkyō and the other big cities like Ōsaka, Kōbe and Nagoya, it is difficult to buy a house close to your work. Tokyoites say that the new housing is 'too far from work, too small and too expensive.' These days if you are lucky enough to be able to afford a home of your own it will usually be well over an hour's train journey from your place of work.

TO COPY INTO YOUR PROJECT BOOK
(filling in the blank spaces).

1. The Japanese tend to live much............together than we do. Many of their houses are............than ours.

2. Japanese children go to play at each other's house, but after lessons and at weekends and holidays they spend time together............

3. The mats made of rice straw that cover floors in Japanese homes are called.............

4. The Japanese always............when they go indoors so that they do not make the tatami dirty.

5. There are two types of sliding screens used in traditional Japanese homes; they are called............and.............

TO TALK ABOUT IN YOUR GROUP

In Japan many people still think that 'the woman's place is in the home.' Do you think this is also true here in your country? In your home are there some jobs which only Mum will do? Only Dad? Only sister/brother....etc.?

What do you consider to be the 'worst' jobs? Who does the 'worst' jobs in your home?

In Japan the husband earns the money and the wife usually decides how to spend it. Who would you say has the most power in the Japanese home? Who controls the money, pays the bills, gives you your pocket-money, in your home? Who has the final word when important decisions are made for your family?

TO FIND OUT AND PREPARE

EITHER:

If you were choosing a new home for your family, what would you look for. Would you want a home in the country? Near to work? Near to a railway station? How large a home would you need? Would you want to rent or buy your home?

OR:

Collect some descriptions of homes from Estate Agents - you might find some in your local newspaper. Write and ask the Estate Agents to send you the plans and descriptions of the new homes they are selling. Perhaps your teacher can arrange for an Estate Agent to come and talk to your class about his or her work. When you have done all your preliminary work, prepare an Estate Agent's brochure of your dream house. This brochure should include a description, pictures, diagrams and a simple plan.

TO WRITE ABOUT AND DESIGN

Some Japanese are not satisfied with their homes. Are you satisfied with the home you live in? What do you think about your home? What do you like best about it? What are the disadvantages of your home - how would you improve things if it were possible? Describe your home now and as it would be changed if you redesigned it. Draw plans to show the changes you would like to make.

Family meal-time (western-style).

Letter 2

12-8-201,
Narashinodai 3,
Funabashi City,
Chiba Prefecture 274,
Japan.

Dear Paul,

Thank you for the nice card and letter. I was so happy to get them. I'm sorry I kept you waiting so long for my answer. I have been very busy.

I will tell you about the place where I live. Did you know that there are four big islands (Hokkaidō, Honshū, Shikoku and Kyūshū) and many smaller islands in Japan? I live on Honshū. If you get a map of Japan (a pretty big one), you will *see* a prefecture called Chiba. It is just east of Tōkyō. Then, look for a town called Funabashi and that is where I live. We call a city like this a 'bed town.' It means a town which is near Tōkyō. There are many people and it is a lively town. The main street is lined with shops. On Sundays or festival days many people come shopping here in Funabashi. There are also many wide parks with green trees. Cherry blossoms are in full bloom in April. I like it here very much.

I will tell you about my house next. I live in a modern concrete and steel building. In my house there are three rooms and a kitchen. I have my own room. My room is *yojōhan* - 4½ mats big. It is a 270 cm square room. In my room there is a steel desk, a piano and a bookcase. I also have a *kotatsu* in my room. A *kotatsu* is a foot warmer put in a recess in the floor. We put our feet in the recess and there is a quilt to keep the warmth in. We put a little portable table on top, and sit round it. But when we are not using the *kotatsu* we put a board over the recess and use the same room for playing, sleeping and for doing anything else. It can be called an 'all purpose room.' Japanese rooms are very convenient.

I have enclosed a picture card. Mt Fuji is the highest mountain in Japan. It is 3,776m high. The flowers which you look at on the card are cherry blossoms. The cherry blossom is the national flower. I like cherry blossoms. I hope you like the picture card.

Well, I've got to go. Have fun!
A Japanese friend.
Sayuri Shimizu

The kotatsu

Opened

Covered with table, quilt and board

TO FIND OUT AND WRITE ABOUT

Why do you think Funabashi is called a 'bed town?' Can you think of any 'bed' or 'dormitory' towns in your country? Use an atlas to help you.

TO FIND OUT AND DRAW

Collect the measurements of your room at home. Measure the length and breadth. Measure the size of your bed, wardrobe, chest of drawers etc. Draw a plan to scale of your bedroom - use the same scale that you used to draw Sayuri Shimizu's room.

TO CALCULATE

Work out how many *tatami* mats would be needed to cover your bedroom. To help with your calculations use the approximate measurements of 2 metres long and 1 metre wide for each mat. (Exact measurements are 1.8 by 0.9 m.)

'Viewing' cherry-blossom in the spring is sometimes a formal occasion.

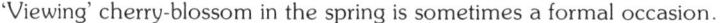

Letter 3

Sakae Shōgakkō,
156 Banchi Funabashi, Ubayachi,
Goshogawara City,
Aomori-ken 037,
Japan.

I am in the 4th year of Sakae Elementary School. I am one of Mr Nomiya's pupils. I will tell you about him. His nick-name is 'thunder' because when he is angry, he is as fearful as the thunder. When he became our class teacher I was very frightened, but as we got to know him, we found he was a very nice and kind teacher.

My school was established in Meiji 10 and has a very old history. Therefore the building is very old and when it rains or when the snow melts, the roof leaks badly. It was bad this winter as it was rather warm. But we enjoyed the warm weather, as we could play in the playground and also it was very easy to get to school. My house is about 2km from school, and I am always frozen to death before I get to school.

Do you have a sports day in the snow? This year, as it was warm, our sports day in the snow was cancelled. I love snow glittering in the sun. I was very disappointed this year that we did not have enough snow and the sports day was cancelled.

In spring we have an ordinary sports day. Our parents always come to that and we have lunch together. Not only the children, but also the parents join in the races and we have a most enjoyable time.

As for our class we have a President, Vice-President and Secretary. Our class is always very cheerful. In our school we select the President, Vice-President and Secretary for 'Jidōkai' (the children's meeting.) It is the time now for us to choose these people and we can see many posters for nominations in the school.

Aomori is famous for its apples. What is your teacher's name? How old is your school? Please let me know about the climate in your country, size of your playground, school events and the famous products of your area - if any.

Do you have snow in winter? We have a lot of snow here and very often we cannot get out of the front door.

GOODBYE

Michiru Fujita

Senior High School students cheering on their baseball team.

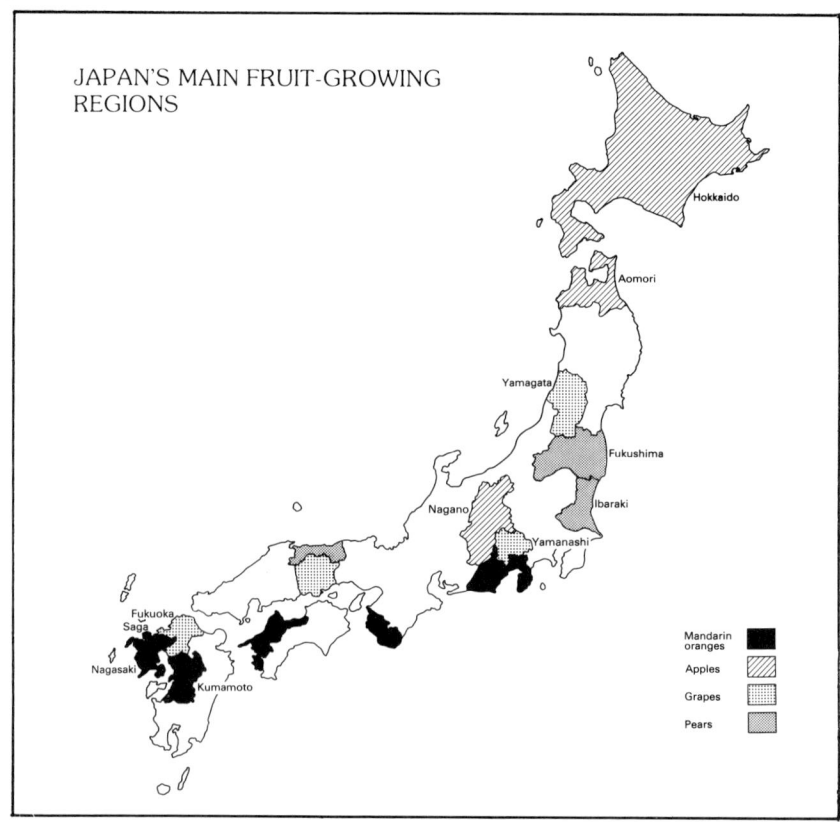

JAPAN'S MAIN FRUIT-GROWING
REGIONS

Hokkaido

Aomori

Yamagata

Fukushima

Ibaraki

Nagano

Yamanashi

Fukuoka
Saga

Nagasaki

Kumamoto

Mandarin
oranges

Apples

Grapes

Pears

TO FIND OUT AND WRITE ABOUT

This letter comes from Michiru Fujita - a ten-year-old boy living on the outskirts of Aomori City. Unlike most of the other letters in this book, this one is a translation. (Most Japanese children do not start learning English until they are 12 years old.) Look at the map of Japan on page 7 and find Aomori. Look also at the 'fruit regions' map opposite. How do you think the climate in Aomori differs from Sayuri's home in Chiba Prefecture?

TO WRITE ABOUT

How do you think most teachers get their nick-names? Write a story about your first day in the class of a new teacher. It might be true or made up or a mixture of the two.

TO PLAN, WRITE AND DESIGN

Imagine that you lived in an area where winter sports days were held every year. Plan the sports day. Make a programme of races - you should include skiing and sledging races and items that you think would help to make the winter sports meeting go well. Are you going to have refreshments? What would be most suitable? Do not forget to design a good cover for your winter sports programme.

TO DISCUSS

What sort of things do you think are discussed at the *Jidōkai*, the childrens' meeting? If there were Council meetings like this at your school, what would you want to talk about - Complaints? Suggestions? Discipline? School Bullies? How would you organise the elections for President? Would you like a secret ballot? Would you have posters advertising the candidates? Why not ask your teacher if you can organise an election for a class President.

TO WRITE ABOUT

Michiru finishes his letter by telling us a little about Aomori, and by asking some questions about your town and school. Try to answer some of his questions - imagine you are writing to Michiru.

FOCUS 2 **Education**

'Education Mama - The Passport to Success'

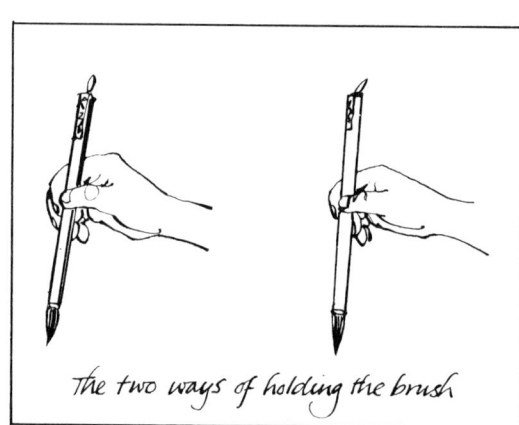

the two ways of holding the brush

Learning to Read and Write

'Nihonjin'
Japanese person

The Japanese writing system is one of the most complicated in the world. Instead of just learning an alphabet of 26 letters, Japanese children have to learn about 2,000 characters (symbols) and two 46-letter alphabets in order to read and write. Much of the time in the first 6 years of a Japanese child's education is spent just memorising. The characters are called *kanji*. The shapes and meanings of these *kanji* were copied from the Chinese language many hundreds of years ago. Japanese is a hard language to learn to read and write, but parents know that it must be mastered if their children are to do well. For this reason mothers often spend hours teaching their children to read and write. Many children make a start on learning to read long before they go to school.

Even though they have one of the most difficult languages in the world to read, the Japanese people read more newspapers than any other nation in the world. (Japan has over 120 daily newspapers with a circulation of nearly 70 million copies, including the evening editions.) There are fewer non-readers in Japan than in Great Britain, Australia or the U.S.A.

The Cost of Education

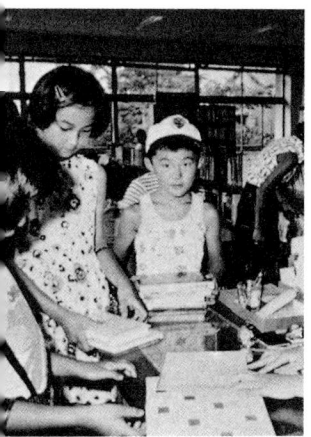

Education is greatly valued in Japan and Japanese parents often describe it as the 'passport to success.' Most parents are prepared to pay for this success. They pay, not only with the time they spend in helping their children, but also with money. Many families pay large fees to private tutors and to private schools. They also have to pay for all education after the age of fifteen. Children do not have to attend school after they are fifteen, but in fact nine out of ten youngsters stay on and go to upper secondary schools for three years (called senior high schools.) About 35% of them go on to colleges or universities when they are eighteen.

Only a small amount (one-fortieth of an average family's earnings) is needed to send a child to a state senior high school - compared with one-sixth of a family's earnings which is needed to send a child to a private secondary school. Even so - seven out of ten parents choose private upper secondary schools for their children.

To send a child to a university medical school, parents have to dig deep into their savings. There is an enormous fee to pay when the student starts, and then parents have to pay as much as a third of a year's earnings each year for tuition. But when they finish their medical training and become qualified doctors, these students belong to one of the highest-paid professions in Japan. Parents of doctors can therefore look forward to a comfortable old age.

The School Day and Examinations

Japanese children have to work hard to keep up with the others in their class, but clever children are encouraged to help their less able classmates. They also do much more homework than children in our country.

From the moment they enter school, Japanese children face many exams. Some children work over six hours each night doing homework. Many have extra lessons from private tutors.

Top: Junior High School girls in their 'sailor' uniform.
Above: The Art lesson. *Right:* Elementary school activities.

Hiroshi Yoshida is fourteen. He leaves for school at 7.45 each morning. He returns home at about 4.30 p.m. and goes straight to bed. His parents wake him at 9.00 p.m. to have a meal with the family, but then he studies through the night until 3 or 4 o'clock in the morning. He then returns to bed to catch a few hours' sleep before getting ready for the next day at school. His parents also pay for four hours' extra maths lessons each weekend.

Westerners who work in Japan often choose to send their children to ordinary Japanese schools. Usually this works quite well until the children are eleven or twelve. Then the children start complaining that they have no friends to play with. Their friends are all studying until late at night. At this age many of the western parents send their children to one of the International Schools instead.

Entrance to University

Japanese parents want their children to study hard so that they will pass all their exams. It is usually the mothers who make the children study. Japanese mothers are often called 'Education Mamas.' Entrance exams decide who goes to which university - and the university a student attends decides where a student goes to work and what job he gets when he graduates.

There are over 450 Japanese universities, but the greatest competition is for the places in the best ones. People who go to these always seem to get the best jobs - the biggest and best companies choose most of their new people from the most prestigious universities. Top people in government and the civil service also usually come from these universities.

Another exam!

TO COPY IN YOUR TOPIC BOOK

(*filling in the blank spaces*)

1. Japanese children have to learn about..........characters and two 46-letter..........in order to read and write.
2. The Japanese read more..........than any other nation in the World. There are fewer..........in Japan than in Great Britain, Australia or the U.S.A.
3. Children do not have to go to school after they are......but 9 out of 10 youngsters stay on to go to......... ....schools.
4. Seven out of ten parents choose to send their children to..........Upper Secondary Schools.
5. It is usually the mothers who make Japanese children study. This is why they are often called.......... ....

TO TALK ABOUT

Why do you think there are fewer non-readers in Japan than in Great Britain, Australia or the U.S.A.?

TO DISCUSS IN YOUR GROUP

In Japan clever children are encouraged to help their less able class-mates. Do you think that this is a good idea? Do you think that these clever children enjoy helping, or would they sooner get on with their own work? Do you think that these less able children like being helped by their friends?

TO TALK ABOUT

What sort of place would you expect Tokyo International School to be? What sort of children would go to this school? What sort of people do you think their parents would be?

'HAPPINESS'

Above: School lunch-time. *Right:*
School cleaning duties.

Letter 4

Kumiko Takebe,
3-5-25-306 Narashinodai,
Chiba City,
Chiba Prefecture,
Japan.

My Dear Friend John,

How do you do? I have been very anxious to have someone to write to in a foreign country. How lucky I am! Yesterday I heard your address from my teacher.

First of all I'll introduce myself. My name is Kumiko which is quite a popular name for girls in Japan. Is John a popular name for boys in your country? I am fourteen years old. I am older than you but I hope you'll not mind it. I was born in Kyōtō on October 13th - so we both have October birthdays. Where were you born?

I go to Narashinodai Junior High School and I'm in the 8th grade. I am going to tell you about my height, weight and some other physical characteristics. I am 5′ 4″ in height and weigh 101 lbs. How tall are you? And how much do you weigh? I'm tall and thin. How about you?

Next I'll tell you about my hobbies. My hobby is collecting stamps, and it is my wish to collect some of the stamps of all the countries of the world. If you have stamps, won't you exchange some of them for Japanese stamps?

You asked me to tell you something about school. As you go to a Primary School I will tell you about the school I used to attend when I was young. Then I will tell you about our Junior High School.

Our Elementary School had about 500 children - from first to sixth grade and all of us lived near school. We shared our school buildings with a kindergarten.

Although we didn't live very far from school my brother and sister always used to go with me. Our route to school was chosen by the police and board of education. They passed it as a safe route. At street corners and busy road crossings there were ladies on duty to make sure we got to school safely. These ladies are called the 'Green Aunties.' They were called that because many years ago they wore green uniforms. I wonder if you have 'Green Aunties' to see you safely to school?

School Rules

Some of our rules were made by teachers and some by the children. Each class or home room sent a representative to the children's committee and the committee made up many of the school rules. Do you have a 'Children's Committee' in your school? Please tell me.

Some of the teachers' rules were:

1. We should not go to school too early. 2. Every pupil must wear the school hat - provided by school - during the journey to and from school.

Do you have rules like these?

We also had rules made up by the pupils at the children's committee. Sometimes they were about the games you could play at playtime - and when you were allowed to play certain types of game. Most of the time the pupils kept these rules much better than the ones made up by the teachers, because we made them ourselves. But some kids broke them. They played ball where they shouldn't. If these boys didn't follow the rules after a warning - then their problem was discussed by the children's committee and the rule breakers' class. We talked about how we could solve the problem.

There were some boys who just wouldn't obey the rules and we didn't know what to do about them. Usually, our classroom teacher would sit quietly at these meetings - listening to our discussions. But if things went wrong and we got angry and had an argument - then he gave us suggestions on how we might settle things.

It wasn't very nice being talked about at the schools' committee.

Cleaning Time

Each day at the end of playtime the bell would ring ꜰ

Bike shed and cleaning materials at a Junior High School.

cleaning time. All the children were very sad to stop their games - and they would take as long as possible before going back indoors. We had to help clean the school. Although we all used vacuum cleaners at home - at school we had to use old-fashioned sweeping brooms and dusters. Some children had never used such things and had to be shown by the teachers or other children the proper way to sweep. We had to wipe the halls and stairs with mops and floor cloths. We had to keep the school clean at all times. Kids in the lower grades seemed to like cleaning.

It's the same at Junior High School. We have to clean there too - but we do not like to do it.

Now I'm going to tell you about Narashinodai Junior High School. It is situated in the city. I go to school on foot. How do you get to school? Our school is a four-storey ferro-concrete building. Our school has more than fifty classrooms and some other rooms with modern equipment - such as a science room and a music room. I hope you will tell me about your school in your next letter.

Volleyball

I don't know exactly how many teachers or students our school has, but it is certain, I may say, that there are more than 1,800 students and more than 60 teachers. Our class has 42 pupils of both sexes. How many pupils and teachers are there in your school?

I'll tell you about my favourite sports. Volleyball is the sport I like best. What sport do you like best?

I don't have any photo of myself now, but I will send you one next time. Won't you send me yours next time too? I'm sending you some stamps which I hope you like. I hope you'll send me some of the beautiful stamps of your country.

Next I'll tell you something about my family. There are five in my family. My parents, a younger brother who is seven, and younger sister, ten and myself. Do you have any brothers and sisters? If so can you please let me know their names. My brother and sister are Masamichi and Shinobu. Mother is kind and sweet and I like her so much, but the only trouble is that she always tells me to study. My father is an office worker, and joking all the time. My father is very earnest about our education.

I finish this letter, looking forward to your reply.

Yours sincerely,

Kumiko Takebe

TO WRITE ABOUT

Kumiko has written a pen portrait describing herself. She has told John about her physical characteristics, her family and her hobbies. Write a description of yourself giving the sort of information that would give a person in a foreign country a very good idea of what you are like.

TO TALK ABOUT

Kumiko asks John to send her some beautiful stamps from his country. If you look through this book you will see that a lot of Japanese stamps have been used as illustrations. The author chose to use stamps because he thought that they give a good picture of some aspects of Japan as a country and the Japanese way of life. It is interesting to see the things the Japanese Post Office chooses to show the world about Japan. If you were responsible for choosing the illustrations for your postage stamps - what would you choose to show the world? What would give a full picture of your country? Think of the achievements, famous people, famous places, great buildings etc. etc. Are there any aspects of life in your country that you would sooner not show the world - some things about which you are not very proud and would not want to show on your stamps?

TO INVESTIGATE

In Japan they have Green Aunties. In Britain they have Lollipop Ladies. Try to find out what arrangements are made in different countries of the world to try and make sure that children get to school safely. You will probably need to write to the Embassies or Tourist Information Offices of the countries you have selected. Discuss with your friends the best way to gather this information. Are you going to assign one pupil to each country? Are you all going to write separate letters? Are you able to use a computer or word processor to help you? Then think of how you are going to present your findings to other people.

TO MAKE INTO A PLAY

Imagine you are all members of a 'Children's Committee.' In the school there are two children who refuse to obey the rules. It had been decided that one part of the playground was for quiet play - no ball games allowed. These two children continually went

Some famous woodblock prints (*see p.92*).

into this quiet area, and yesterday during their ball game they knocked over and hurt one of the youngest children. What are you going to do in 'Children's Committee?' How are you going to solve the problem?

TO DISCUSS IN CLASS

Kumiko seems to suggest that the pupils who broke rules in her school were always boys. Do you think girls are better behaved than boys? Why does it sometimes seem like that? Try and give reasons for your opinions.

TO CALCULATE

Find out how long it takes to clean your school each week. Find out how many cleaners are employed - and how long they work each day. Make a list of all the jobs they have to do and how long they spend on each task. Show your results as a graph. Think carefully about how you are going to get your information.

FOCUS 3   **Fortune-telling**

'Snake People are neat and tidy...'

Fortune teller

Having one's fortune told is very popular in Japan. Fortune-tellers can be found in town centres and at temples where visitors pay to have their fortunes told. In the temples the usual way to buy a fortune is by shaking a box holding numbered rods. When a rod falls out of the box it is examined and the number read off. The customer is then given a piece of paper (bearing the same number) with a fortune written on it.

At temples it is usually the custom to tie good fortunes on to a nearby tree, or to the temple gate - to make them come true. Often bad fortunes are also tied up - to make them disappear!

If you speak to Japanese people about fortunes and fortune-telling they will tell you that they are not true believers - they just think of it as superstition and harmless fun. However, few people get married without first consulting a fortune-teller. Most who admit to being 'true believers' are among the elderly and unmarried young people.

The Japanese zodiac was brought from China, along with a

Ema (wooden tablets) are found at all temples and shrines; people write wishes on them and hang them up in the hope that their wish will come true. Printed fortunes are also tied to a nearby tree for the same reason.

religion called Buddhism, in about 400 A.D. Part of the folklore about the zodiac is the story that long ago Buddha, the founder of Buddhism, called all the animals to him. He said that those that came would be given a reward - a year would be named after them. Of all the animals in the world - only 12 came. They came in this order: the rat, the ox, the tiger, the rabbit, the dragon, the snake, the horse, the ram, the monkey, the bird, the dog and the boar. As time went by the belief grew among the Japanese people that their personality and fortune were related to the character of the animal governing the year in which they were born. Today, Japanese people still feel that their life is influenced by their birth sign, although, like many of us who read our horoscopes in newspapers and magazines, it is usually treated as fun and not taken too seriously.

The order in which the animals appear in any 12-year cycle is always the same. The present cycle began in 1984 with the year of the Rat. (Obviously, the cycles before that began in 1972, 1960, 1948, 1936 and so on. This will help you work out the zodiac sign for your parents, grandparents and other older people you know.) By the way, when asked their age, some Japanese people prefer to say which animal they are rather than tell their age straight out. They leave the calculation to the questioner.

The following characteristics are usually connected with people born in the given years.

YEAR OF THE RAM (e.g. 1955, 1967, 1979, 1991)

People born in the year of the Ram are usually thin and shy. They tend to expect the worst things in life. Often life is a puzzle for them and they are not sure what plans they should make. They are timid people - not leaders. Because they are uncertain about themselves and what they should do, Ram-year people must be guided and led by others.

These wise and gentle people are often sentimental and feel pity for those less fortunate than themselves. Rams are the great givers to charity - often they are far too embarrassed about their generosity to want any thanks.

Ram people are often good at arts and crafts. Although they will not expect it, life will be kind to them and they will never have to worry about food or clothes or a home. A Ram's talents always make money easy to get.

Rams should marry either a Rabbit-year person, a Boar-year person or a Horse-year person. A bad marriage would be with someone born in the year of the Rat, Ox or Dog.

YEAR OF THE MONKEY (e.g. 1956, 1968, 1980, 1992)

People born in the year of the Monkey are usually alert, clever and impatient. They are very inventive and are able to solve difficult problems easily.

Monkey people like to do things for others, but they do not make many friends. Often they are conceited and boastful and have a poor opinion of those less gifted than themselves. Monkey-year people are the hard workers who are always eager to learn more, to read, to see and to know.

Monkey people should marry someone born in the year of the Dragon or Rat. A bad marriage would be with someone born in the year of the Snake, Boar or Tiger.

YEAR OF THE BIRD (e.g. 1957, 1969, 1981, 1993)

People born in the year of the Bird are schemers and planners. They are always busy and love hard work. Indeed, often they take on so much that nothing ever gets finished. Bird people always feel that they are right and that others are wrong. Because of this they have no trust in other people. Although they appear to always have great plans and grand ideas - most of these ideas seem to fade away to nothing.

Others find Bird-year people interesting - but that does not mean that they always like them.

Bird people should marry people born in the year of the Ox, Snake or Dragon. Bad marriages would be with those born in the years of the Rabbit, Dog, Bird or Rat.

YEAR OF THE DOG (e.g. 1958, 1970, 1982, 1994)

These people are very loyal and absolutely honest. They often inspire others and are reliable about keeping secrets. However, they are very stubborn and can have quite cruel tongues.

People born in the year of the Dog do not really seem to bother about money and yet they seem to get all the money they need. These are the people who are determined to see fair play - those who do not rest until justice has been done.

People born in these years make good, hard-working and honest leaders. In many cases Dog-year women are very attractive.

Dog-year people should marry people born in the year of the Horse, Tiger and Rabbit. A bad marriage would be with one born in the year of the Dragon or Ram.

YEAR OF THE BOAR (e.g. 1959, 1971, 1983, 1995)

These people are full of determination. When they set out to do something, nothing will make them change their mind. These honest, patient people do not make many friends, but when they do they make friends for life. They do not talk much either - but when they do talk it is because they have something worth saying.

Boar people are often quite short-tempered and yet they hate arguments. They are affectionate and kind to their loved ones.

If a Boar person has a problem, he or she will usually try and solve it for themselves - indeed they will find it almost impossible to ask for help. Boar men are self-confident. The women have a good sense of humour and will often make all the decisions for the household. Because of this Boar-year people should not marry others born in the same year. A Snake person would also be a very bad marriage. The best choice would be any of those born in the year of the Rat, Ox, Tiger, Dragon, Horse, Bird or Dog.

YEAR OF THE RAT (e.g. 1960, 1972, 1984, 1996)

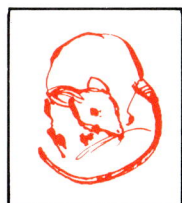

These people are clever and cheerful and full of charm. However, they are often fussy about silly little details and can be rather mean.

Unfortunately, they may waste what they hoard by spending it on someone they love but who does not love them. Apart from this the only thing they really like is to spend their money on themselves.

Rat people allow themselves to lose their tempers very easily and yet if they wish they can control themselves very well. These people love to chatter and gossip, and because of this they tend not to keep their friends for long.

The best choice for marriage would be to someone born in the year of the Dragon, Monkey or Ox. The worst choice would be to one born in the year of the Horse. A popular superstition is that a Rat-year man marrying a Horse-year woman dies young!

YEAR OF THE OX (e.g. 1961, 1973, 1985, 1997)

These people are normally very gentle, patient and quiet. However, for all their patience, when they are really angered they are best avoided for their rage is tremendous.

Ox people are very clever with their hands. They are very stubborn and hate to fail at anything they set their mind to. Slow but sure seems to be the motto of these people. Men seem to take a long time to grow up - women are careful and good home-keepers.

Marriage for people born in the Ox year is rather strange - for most of them do not really love anyone very much. Because they are so cool the best type of marriage would be to someone born in the Snake, Bird or Rat year. A bad marriage would be with one in the year of the Ram, Dog or Horse.

YEAR OF THE TIGER (e.g. 1962, 1974, 1986, 1998)

Tiger people are sensitive, sympathetic and short-tempered. They are very fond of their families.

Often other people give Tiger people more credit than they deserve as they appear to be very wise and intelligent. However, they are often narrow-minded and suspicious of other people and often they delay too long when making important decisions.

These people can be very selfish and mean and yet in Japan it is thought to be very fortunate to be born in the year of the Tiger. Tiger people are supposed to be the protectors of life - protectors against thieves, fire and ghosts.

The women born in this year are very good at working with their husbands.

Horse-year, Dragon-year and Dog-year people make the best spouses for Tiger-born people. The worst marriage for a Tiger person would be with either a Snake-year or a Monkey-year person.

YEAR OF THE RABBIT (e.g. 1963, 1975, 1987, 1999)

These scrupulously clean people are quiet and gentle. They glide through life making no enemies and few real friends. They are smooth talkers, hard workers and are trusted by just about everyone.

Rabbit people are talented and ambitious and other people greatly admire them. In money affairs Rabbit people do well.

These people lead peaceful lives with few real ups and downs. If they have a fault, it is in their fondness for gossip and idle chatter.

Some Japanese people are suspicious of Rabbit-year people as they believe that witches sometimes take this form.

Rabbit people would do well to marry someone born in the year of the Ram, Boar or Dog. Bad marriages would be with Rat- or Bird-year people.

YEAR OF THE DRAGON (e.g. 1964, 1976, 1988, 2000)

Dragon people are healthy and full of energy. They are short-tempered and stubborn, honest, sensitive and brave.

Dragon people are a strange mixture of opposites. They are fighters and dreamers. They have many opportunities while young and yet they are often unlucky in later life. They are capable of doing good work and devoting themselves to good causes, but they can be just as energetic in devoting themselves to evil.

Dragon people often talk too much. They say a great deal that they do not mean just because they do not know how to keep quiet.

Dragon men are often so generous and extravagant that their showing-off leads to ruin. The women, too, are fond of dressing up and showing off.

Dragon people often worry a great deal and often for no good reason. They tend to take a long time before marrying, and in many cases they do not marry at all.

The best marriage for a Dragon person would be with a person born in the year of the Rat, Snake, Monkey or Bird. The worst would be with one born in the year of the Dog, Ox, Rabbit or Dragon.

YEAR OF THE SNAKE (e.g. 1965, 1977, 1989, 2001)

People born in the year of the Snake are neat and tidy. They are very patient and are capable of putting up with terrible hardships. They speak little but have great wisdom. They are kind and loving and are often idolised by others.

They are very determined people and hate to fail at anything. Although they are always calm they are absolutely obsessed with success.

People born in the year of the snake are handsome if they are men and beautiful if they are women. These people are quite conceited and love fine clothes.

Snake people love helping others - even when the person does not need or want help.

Best marriages are with those born in the year of the Ox or Bird. The worst marriage would be with a person born in the year of the Tiger or Boar.

YEAR OF THE HORSE (e.g. 1966, 1978, 1990, 2002)

People born in the year of the Horse are bright and cheerful but it is often said that they talk too much. They are hopeless at keeping secrets. They are popular with others and are clever at paying compliments. Horse-year people are clever at making things. They are quick thinkers and look after money well. However, they have the fault of not being able to stick at things for any long period of time. They become bored far too easily.

Horse-year people seem to be show-offs both in dress and behaviour - but really they are rather shy particularly with members of the opposite sex. They can be quick-tempered and are not known for their patience. Horse-year people are very independent and do not very often listen to advice - even if it is good.

The best marriages for those born in the year of the Horse would be with those born in the year of the Tiger, Dog or Sheep. A bad marriage would be to someone born in the year of the Ox, Rabbit or Horse. The worst marriage of all would be with one born in the year of the Rat.

TO COPY IN YOUR TOPIC BOOK

(filling in the blank spaces)

1. Having one's.........told is far more..........in Japan than in Great Britain or the U.S.A. or Australia or other 'western' countries.
2. If you speak to most Japanese people about fortunes and fortune-telling, they will tell you that they are not..........they just think of it as..........and.......... ....
3. The Japanese zodiac was introduced to the country around..........from...........
4. Long ago Buddha called all the..........to him. Of all the..........in the world only..........came to him.
5. The animals who came to Buddha were the.........., ...,
.........., ..., ..., ..., ..., ..., ..., ...,
.... and the........... They were all rewarded by having a..........named after them.

TO INVESTIGATE AND WRITE ABOUT

Do you ever look at the 'Stars' or 'Horoscopes' in newspapers or magazines? Why do you think that people all over the world seem to be interested in the stars and fortune-telling? Try to collect as many newspapers as you can that tell the stars, and compare the information given by each astrologer. Do they all say the same thing or do they vary? Write a review of your birth star for a given day, showing what different astrologers say.

TO WRITE ABOUT

Look again at the animals of the Japanese zodiac. Now choose the animal which represents the year of birth of your brother, sister, mother or father. Read carefully the characteristics described. Do you think that this description gives a true picture of what they are like as people? What characteristics are accurate? What characteristics are untrue?

TO WRITE ABOUT

Imagine that 13 animals were honoured by Buddha. Pick a 13th animal and write a fortune for people born in the Year of the ....

TO FIND OUT AND RECORD

Make a graph showing the birth stars of the people in your class. Are there more people born at any one time of the year? How many Capricorns or Libras are there? Compare your class with another in the school to check if the same star sign is the most popular.

TO WRITE AND ILLUSTRATE

Write and illustrate a story about a Monkey-year person and his or her Ox-year friend. Tell of some of the adventures they have. What sort of friendship do you think it would be? What sort of things might they argue about?

TO JOIN IN

This is an activity in which all the class can take part. Split up into groups of about 5 or 6. Sit round in a circle. Now take it in turns within your group to say positive things about each member of your group. It will mean that everyone will receive 4 or 5 favourable comments. After you have finished the game write down the good things that were said about you and compare these comments with the animal zodiac descriptions.

TO WRITE ABOUT

Read the fortune for your birth year once again. Do you think this is a good description of you? Write about what you are really like.

TO MAKE

In Japan at some temples it is the custom to tie good fortunes to a nearby tree. Why not make a 'Wishing Tree' in your classroom? You could find a large bare branch and hang it up in your classroom. You and your friends could write a wish on a piece of paper and tie it to your 'Wishing Tree.'

THE SEVEN GODS OF FORTUNE

The Seven Gods of Fortune are deified at many shrines and are bought as popular souvenirs throughout Japan.

Ebisu
wealth & fishing

Daikoku
productivity

Benten
music, beauty

Fukuroku
wealth & long life

Bishamon
warriors

Hotei
fortune

Jurojin
longevity

FOCUS 4   **A Japanese Folk Story**

A Tale of Two Wens

Long ago, high up in the Japanese mountains, lived some wood-cutters and their families.

Two of the woodcutters had wens on their cheeks (a wen is a lump.) One woodcutter's lump was on his right cheek. He was called Migi, which means right. The other's lump was on his left cheek and his name was Hidari, which means left.

Neither of the men liked having these lumps, which were as big as apples. In fact, both men spent a lot of time and money trying to get rid of them. Migi, the one whose lump was on the right cheek, was patient and cheerful and he seldom complained. Even so, he sometimes wished that a clever doctor would make his wen disappear.

Hidari was very different. He was a jealous person and he greatly envied everyone he knew. Not surprisingly, he had hardly any friends and he was very unpopular with the other woodcutters. Only Migi and his wife showed any kindness towards him.

One day, when the woodcutters were out in the forest, a great thunderstorm began. Immediately they scattered in all directions in search of shelter. Migi was separated from the others, but he did not mind for he quickly found cover in a hollow tree. The rain continued to fall steadily and Migi curled up and fell asleep.

Although the rain eventually stopped - Migi slept on. It was not until the day was ending that he woke up and peered out from inside the tree.

As he was about to leave his shelter, he heard the sound of approaching footsteps. Naturally, he thought it was the other woodcutters who had come to look for him and he was looking forward to going home. How soon his hopes turned to fears! As the footsteps came nearer he could see that they did not belong to his friends. They belonged to the demons of the night.

Migi's teeth chattered with fear as the creatures came nearer and nearer to his hiding place. Each demon was different from the other - and all were very ugly. One had only one eye and that was in the middle of its face. Another, with the face of a monkey had no mouth. Many seemed as large as giants. Some had hooves like goats.

The demons gathered in a circle in front of Migi's tree. Then one of the creatures began to play a flute, and the sounds of strange sad music filled the forest. How strange, thought Migi, that a creature so ugly could produce such a beautiful sound.

As the demon played the others danced. On and on they danced - never breaking their circle.

Migi decided that he could wait no longer. He must be brave. After much hesitation he stepped out from the hollow tree and bowed to the demons.

'See a human creature! Look! Look!' the demons yelled.

'Who are you, and what do you want?' they asked him.

'I am Migi, the woodcutter with a lump on my right cheek,' he answered, bowing even lower this time.

'And a splendid lump it is too!' croaked the leader of the demons. How happy Migi felt. Never before had anyone, not even his wife, referred to his lump as being splendid.

'Come and join us. Can you dance?' asked the one-eyed creature.

'My friends, I only know one dance. It is called the Woodcutters' Dance.'

'Dance it, dance it! Show us!' they shrilled and croaked and shouted.

Migi bowed to the leader and left the circle to fetch his axe and saw. Holding the axe in his right hand and the saw in his left, he danced for his new friends.

Such a dance he had never danced before. Each step was perfect. Each movement a delight.

'Hurrah!'

'Well done!'

'A marvellous dance!'

'You must teach it to us.'

'Tomorrow, tomorrow,' said the leader. 'Daylight is coming. We must be gone.'

'You must promise that you will come back tomorrow and teach us your dance,' demanded the demons.

'I promise,' said Migi.

'No! You must leave something of value behind, so that you will be sure to return,' said the musician of the group.

'Yes. What's the best thing for him to leave with us?' asked another demon.

Quickly the group of creatures huddled together, but before they could decide the leader yelled - 'I've got it! I've got it! I've never seen a human with such a marvellous wen. That's it, we'll take his lump and then he will certainly return tomorrow.'

To Migi's amazement the leader reached out his hand and plucked the wen from his cheek as easily as picking a ripe apple from a tree.

The woodcutter was near to tears with joy. He felt no pain and hurriedly searched his face for signs of scars. There were none. When he turned to his demon friends, they had vanished.

Migi raced home as fast as his tired legs could carry him. His wife was waiting for him as he approached their little cottage, for she had been worried for his safety.

As they met his wife spluttered 'Your... you've lost your.... How is it possible? Oh, how happy I am for you.' They entered their little home and Migi told his wife the whole story. As they settled to a happy, peaceful meal there was a knock at the door. It was Hidari.

You can imagine Hidari's reaction when he too saw Migi's face. He was not at all happy for his friend's good fortune. No, he was immediately very jealous indeed.

'How did you get rid of your lump?' he demanded.

Migi told the whole story again and Hidari listened eagerly. When he heard how Migi's lump had been painlessly taken from him as a pledge to return, he begged Migi to allow him to return in his place.

It was agreed and next day Hidari set off on his journey.

Hidari found the hollow tree easily. Migi's directions had been good. However, there was no sign of the demons. Hidari was impatient. He moaned at having to wait. Hours later, he was still grumbling to himself. Suddenly he was shaking with excitement. Creatures appeared from nowhere and began dancing. It was just as Migi had described.

Nervously Hidari stepped forward.

'Who is it? Look!' cried the creatures.

'Don't worry - it is the woodcutter who has returned just as he promised,' said the demon chief.

'Thank you for coming. Now dance for us again.'

Hidari stood up and began to dance. However, unlike Migi, he was a poor dancer. He had never bothered with such things as dancing. He thought that anything would do to please these ugly demons, so he just hopped about, waving his arms and stamping his feet.

The creatures just stared in disbelief at this appalling display. 'How badly he dances today' muttered the leader. Finally he could bear it no longer. 'Your performance today is quite different from the dance of yesterday. We don't want to see any more!' he announced. 'However, just to show you that we are not as bad as some people make out, we will give your splendid lump back. Now go away at once!'

THE STORY OF 'THE DWARF'

With these words he took the lump, which he had taken from Migi the day before, and threw it at the right cheek of Hidari. Immediately it took root. It was as if it had grown there always, and all attempts to pull it off were useless. Instantly the demons vanished. Now Hidari was doubly miserable.

On his return home, Hidari locked himself in his hut for two days. He felt ashamed. He feared the laughing and the mocking of his neighbours.

On the third day Migi and his wife called on the lonely woodcutter. Hidari, shamefully opened the door. The couple entered and were greatly upset at Hidari's misfortune. They did not laugh at the man with two lumps. This surprised Hidari so much, that he almost forgot about his two wens during the happy evening he spent with his two friends.

No one knows if Hidari ever lost either of his lumps but it is said that he gradually lost his bad temper and jealousy.

TO BRAINSTORM AND DISCUSS

What are the qualities of a true friend? A true friend is...........

TO TALK ABOUT

Why did people tell stories like this? Can you think of any other stories about unselfish people, or jealous people?

TO DESIGN

Make a comic strip which tells the story of 'A Tale of Two Wens.'

TO WRITE ABOUT

Look at the pictures of the three stamps (opposite page) that tell the story 'THE DWARF.' Stamp 1 is called 'Sailing in a Wooden Boat.' Stamp 2 'Conquering the Goblins,' and Stamp 3 'Wielding the Magic Mallet.' Make up your own 'folk tale' that could use these pictures as the illustrations.

Letter 5

1-4-3-502 Akitsu,
Narashino City,
Chiba Prefecture,
275 Japan.

Dear Janine,

Thank you for telling me about your home in Oxspring and Sheffield so well. I think Oxspring is beautiful, and Sheffield is a big city.

My own area is a reclamation place, part of Tōkyō Bay. My house is on the 5th floor. There is a big shopping centre 10km away. It has 300 shops and is the biggest shopping centre in Japan. The name is Lalaport. Two thousand cars can park there. I go to Lalaport sometimes. Tōkyō Disneyland is also nearby. Sometimes we go shopping in Lalaport. We go by bicycle or by car.

I joined the Akitsu Soccer Club. I play soccer every Sunday from 8.00 - 11.00 a.m.

After school I study with some friends in my house or in the house of a friend, and after we play outdoor games.

I was ranked second in the marathon for my class. I was very happy. I came 4th in school.

From your friend,

Takashi

TO TALK ABOUT

There are a number of things to discuss in this letter. What do you think is a reclamation area? Is there anything that you find surprising in this letter?

FOCUS 5   **Sports and Games**

Jūdō means 'The Gentle Way'

The Japanese like to play all kinds of sports, but baseball is the most popular for both youngsters and adults alike and attracts a lot of spectator interest throughout Japan. Baseball is played at all levels in Japan - there are school teams, amateur baseball clubs and professional baseball leagues. There are two six-club professional baseball leagues in Japan - the Central and the Pacific. They play games regularly between April and October in stadia in all the major cities.

Like soccer in Europe, baseball has many enthusiastic supporters and the leading players are as famous as film and pop stars.

Soccer, too, has been a firmly-established favourite for many years. Also popular are volleyball, tennis, table-tennis and swimming with rugby and basketball fast becoming the new favourites with students and young people.

Golf has developed into the fastest-growing sport of all. Until a few years ago it was regarded as a rich man's game, but now millions play golf. There are over 2000 golf courses. Even so, because of the cost, few people who play golf can afford to use normal golf courses unless their company pays for them; most players have to be satisfied with multi-storey golf driving ranges.

Land costs in Japan are so high that in large towns and cities multi-storey and basement golf ranges are commonplace. It might not be possible to lay a full-scale golf course down in Tōkyō, but office building roofs, unused basements and even the 1964 Olympic Stadium are used as places to improve golfing skills.

Of the winter sports, skiing and skating are the most popular. Japan has many suitable mountain sites combined with an ideal climate for winter sports. There are 12 million skiers and skaters and of these 40% are women.

The combination of ideal weather conditions and a variety of mountain ranges has also aroused a growing interest in mountaineering. Now there are many active alpine clubs wherever there are mountains to be climbed!

Traditional sports in Japan also have a large and growing following. They include 'Sumō,' 'Jūdō' and 'Kendō.'

Girls also take a keen interest in baseball and karate.

Sumō

Sumō is a form of wrestling where the winner is the one who forces his opponent to the ground or out of the ring. A wrestler is 'out' even if he just touches the ground with his hand. A Sumō wrestling match is a combination of physical power, showmanship, skill and ritual. The average weight of a wrestler is around 280 pounds (20 stone). The wrestlers perform a lengthy and symbolic ritual before the contest and yet the action is usually over in seconds. Sumō is a highly professional sport with the top-ranked wrestlers enjoying considerable acclaim and financial reward. Sumō competitions have a tremendous following with live television coverage and many action replays and repeats. The beginnings of Sumō go back to the eighth century A.D.

Action shots from Jūdō practice (*left*) and a Sumō tournament (*above*).

Jūdō is a form of self-defence which requires quick action and great skill rather than just physical strength or size. The mental, physical and self-defence aspects of Jūdō were quickly recognised in Japan and it rapidly grew in popularity. It is still a very popular option in Japanese schools. Jūdō has now spread to all parts of the world. Jūdō means 'the gentle way.'

A Kendō competition.

Kendō

Kendō is a form of fencing. It is one of the most difficult of Japanese martial arts. Two contestants - both wearing protective gear, attack each other with bamboo swords. There are many complicated rules and regulations. It is a sport based on the old sword fighting methods of the *samurai* - the warriors of the feudal age. Many years ago the *samurai* substituted bamboo sticks for their long and deadly steel swords, so that they could practise their sword-fighting techniques without killing anyone. Today, Kendō is one of the most popular martial arts and like Jūdō, it is often taught in schools.

The Japanese are very keen on sport and usually take their practice very seriously. They like competition very much indeed and are also enthusiastic spectators.

TO COPY IN YOUR TOPIC BOOK

(filling in the blank spaces)

1. ....is the most popular sport in Japan for both..........and..........alike.
2. The two professional baseball leagues in Japan are the..........and the...........
3. The fastest growing sport in Japan is...........
4. Jūdō is a form of self-defence based on quick action and great skill rather than..........or...........
5. Kendō is a sport based on the old sword fighting methods of the...........

TO INVESTIGATE AND REPORT

Out of all the sports in Japan, why do you think baseball is the most popular? Find out as much as you can about the game and how it is played.

TO PLAN, DESIGN AND WRITE ABOUT

Sports of all kinds continue to attract more and more people of all ages who wish to pursue them. Design a Sports Centre that will accommodate many sports within a limited space.

TO DISCUSS

In Japan, the most important baseball games are shown live on T.V. Outside Japan, especially in Britain, some people have suggested that showing games live on T.V. is the reason why fewer people have been going to watch the match at the ground. Is it important that there is a crowd at the ground - or is it enough that millions watch on T.V.?

TO INVESTIGATE AND DESIGN

Try to find out about one of the Japanese martial arts. Make an illustrated booklet about the 'art' you choose.

FOCUS 6　**Leisure and Entertainment**

Kantō Television Programmes

Kantō is the name of the Tōkyō region of Japan.

9.02 p.m. U.S. Movie: — "Extreme Prejudice" dubbed into Japanese.'

(A U.S. film about two boyhood friends; one a Texas Ranger and the other a Drug Smuggler.)

Studio production of a TV drama at the Japan Broadcasting Corporation (NHK).

Leisure at Home

Watching television is the most popular leisure activity for the Japanese. Nearly 100% of all households in Japan have television sets. Over two-thirds of homes have more than one television set. Similarly, well over half of all households own a video cassette recorder. There are over 7,000 television stations and nearly 1,000 radio stations. Broadcasting in Japan is local -

a station serves only a limited area - perhaps a town and the countryside around it. Most homes are able to receive quite a high number of stations. Satellite T.V. is already very popular in Japan and is expanding rapidly. Over half of the television and three-quarters of the radio stations are controlled by Nippon Hōsō Kyōkai (N.H.K.) - Japan Broadcasting Corporation. This is a public corporation that is very similar to the B.B.C. in Britain and the A.B.C. in Australia.

The Japanese enjoy reading. There are over 120 different daily newspapers and over 50 million copies are printed each day. On average, every family in Japan takes about two newspapers per day. In addition, there are many local papers, sports papers and over 2,600 different magazines on the market.

The Japanese book and magazine industry is one of the largest in the world. Very few Japanese publications are sold abroad. Books and magazines are relatively inexpensive and as a result approximately 50 magazines are bought by each person per year. Children and adults also read many comic-books.

Traditional Domestic Arts

Cha no yu (the Tea Ceremony)

The tea ceremony is a traditional form of art originally performed by Buddhist monks. It is still taught to many young women before they marry. The host or hostess prepares and serves green tea to a small number of guests. The utensils used in the tea-making are very simple, yet they are beautifully made. The tea room is also very simple: it is decorated with only a scroll and a flower arrangement. The ceremony is a ritual of movement and contemplation. If it is performed well, the participants achieve a peaceful state of mind. They also appreciate the beauty in performing simple tasks, and have peace and quiet to enjoy the craftsmanship of the handmade utensils.

Ikebana (Flower Arranging)

The Japanese tradition of flower arranging also began in Buddhist temples. Flowers, usually lotus blooms, were presented as offerings to Buddha. In modern *ikebana* many different materials such as flowers, leaves, berries, branches, bark, stones and sand are used - but many arrangements concentrate

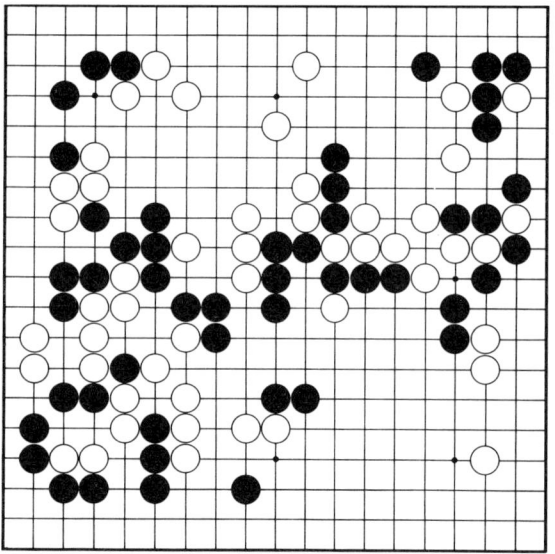

Japanese housewives learn the art of Tea Ceremony. *Above left:* A Tea Master demonstrates the art of using the Tea Ceremony implements. *Left:* The game of *Go*.

on showing off just one bloom to perfection. The aim of this type of flower arranging is to emphasise simplicity and harmony. Today, it is very popular with women, though some men practise it too, as was the case in earlier times.

Go (Japanese Board Game)

Go is a popular pastime with families. It is played on a square board divided by 19 lines horizontally and vertically. Only two people can play. At first sight, it seems an easy game to play. The two participants take it in turn to place a black or white stone on the intersections of the lines on the board. The aim is to capture territory by creating islands with your stones. If you are able to surround your opponent's stones you gain possession of them. The winner is the player who has the most territory at the end of the game.

Like chess, there are many strategies and tactics to learn in order to become a skilled player. Some people become so good that they are able to make their living as professional 'Go' players.

Entertainment

The Cinema

Japan has been making films since 1899. Before the Second World War, many films were made, but were not often shown outside Japan. During the war, a large number of cinemas and studios were destroyed. These were rebuilt after 1946 and the rapid development of the film industry made Japan one of the world's leading film-makers. Between 1950 and 1960 many first-class films were made which gained international awards. Since 1960, the number of people going to the cinema has declined due to the increasing popularity of television.

Scene from *The Seven Samurai*, one of Japan's classic films.

The Theatre

Noh mask

Japan has three forms of traditional theatre. All are very different from western drama.

Noh is the oldest form of theatre in Japan. It began over 600 years ago and used to be performed in the open air outside shrines and temples. The modern Noh theatre has a stage shaped like an inverted L and it is covered by a roof. The only piece of scenery is a backcloth on which is painted an old pine tree. Musicians sit at the back of the stage and a chorus sits on the right-hand side.

A Noh play is a dance-drama. The actors chant and dance their parts. The orchestra marks the rhythm of the dance and creates the atmosphere. The songs of the chorus explain the setting or the feelings of the characters. The main character in a Noh play always wears a mask and his clothes are made of beautiful fabrics. Usually this character represents a ghost or a spirit. In the past, the Noh programme consisted of five plays but now there are just three. The order of the plays is very important. The first one is an introduction and is about gods and happiness. The second one is the most important. It is usually about famous people such as warriors, beautiful young women or someone who is mad. The final play, the conclusion, is about supernatural beings. The costumes are vivid and the action is slow although there are some dramatic moments.

Bunraku puppet and backers

Bunraku is the Japanese puppet theatre. Puppets are popular among children all over the world but the Bunraku is unlike any of the puppet shows seen in the West. The puppets are large - usually about half life size. They usually weigh between 6 and 20 kgs. The puppets are not operated from behind the scenes like our puppets. The puppeteers, who stand behind the stage are visible to the audience from the waist upwards. However, they wear black cloaks and hoods to make themselves appear invisible. (It is a convention of Japanese theatre that if a person is dressed all in black - then that person does not exist. People who move furniture or change the set are usually dressed in black for this reason.) The puppets are cleverly made. The parts within the head all move and the limbs bend at the joints. Each puppet is operated by three people. The leading puppeteer works the right arm, the neck and the head. He supports the weight of the puppet with his left arm and works its features with his fingers. One assistant operates the left arm and has to follow the leader very carefully; the other assistant works the legs.

In Bunraku, the tayū or story-teller and the shamisen player are

Above: Scene from a Noh play. *Below:* scene from a Kabuki play.

as important as the puppets. The *tayū* tells the story which is in the form of a poem. It is half chanted, half sung. The *tayū* has to use different voices to distinguish the characters and also to express their moods. The shamisen player not only accompanies the narration but also creates the atmosphere for the play.

Kabuki is a more popular form of traditional Japanese theatre. Ordinary people still attend this type of theatre whereas it is usually only the intellectuals who are attracted to Noh theatre.

On entering the Kabuki theatre, the first thing that catches the eye is the curtain. It is made up of vertical stripes in three colours - black, green and tan. The Kabuki stage extends across the back of the theatre and has a gangway leading out through the audience on the left. This is called the flower-walk. The main stage is able to revolve in order to change the scene. The chorus sits to the right of the stage and the musicians to the left. The main instrument in the band is the shamisen, a three-stringed instrument played with a plectrum. Flutes, drums and wooden clappers are also used to help create the atmosphere.

Scene from *Chushingura*, one of the great Kabuki stories.

There are over 300 plays written for the Kabuki theatre. Many of them were originally written for the Bunraku theatre. The most famous Kabuki playwright was Chikamatsu Monzaemon who lived over 300 years ago. He is sometimes called Japan's Shakespeare.

Kabuki plays are of three different types: there are dance-dramas in which the actors move to the accompaniment of vocal and instrumental music, historical dramas about nobles and warriors, and dramas about everyday people and their lives.

Actresses are not allowed to take part in Kabuki plays. Female characters are played by men. The men who specialise in taking women's roles spend many years training for these parts. Most Kabuki actors are specialists. They are known for the way they play one type of character, an old man, a foolish person, a rogue and so on.

Music

Shamisen

Koto

J apanese 'Pop' stars are just as popular as stars the world over. There are solo singers, groups, folk singers and jazz groups, and the Top 20 charts are just as important to Japanese young people as they are to us. While many American and British groups have hits in Japan, there are also many home-based groups singing in Japanese. While some of these imitate the more popular western groups, there are more and more performers that are trying to be original.

Western classical music is also very popular. There are many symphony orchestras that play the great works of famous composers such as Beethoven and Bach. Recently Japanese classical composers have become internationally recognised. The best known of these is Takemitsu who is acknowledged throughout the world.

As well as this classical music which came to Japan from Europe, there is also Japan's own traditional music. To our ears much of this music may seem strange. Traditional Japanese instruments include the koto, the shamisen and the shakuhachi. (See illustrations.)

Pachinko

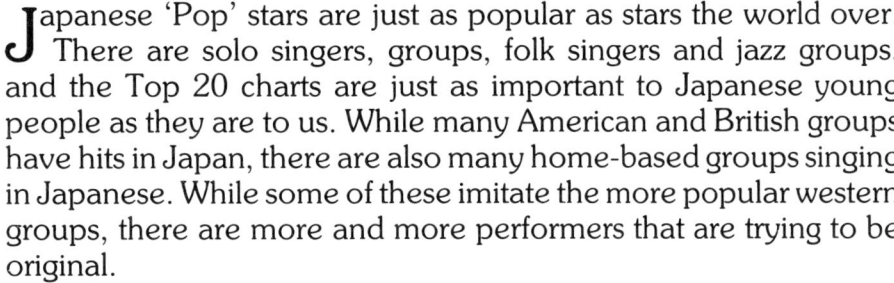

Pachinko

P achinko is a type of pinball game. It is played in noisy, brightly-lit parlours in the centres of Japanese cities. At the entrance, a player buys a tray of small metal balls. These are fed into the machine and shot at one of eight cups. If a player manages to get a ball into a cup, the machine will pay out more balls. These can be used in another game or exchanged at the desk for prizes of cigarettes, chocolates, groceries or a household item. Most players drop into these parlours on their way home from work or on a shopping trip. A few people have tried to become professional pachinko players by exchanging their prizes for cash. This is now illegal. The Japanese Government has been very anxious to reduce the popularity of pachinko and so they have brought in new laws about the value of prizes and opening hours. They have also refused to renew the licences of many pachinko parlours.

It is said that some pachinko parlours are owned by Japanese gangsters - the Yakuza. The Japanese Government is not anti-gambling - it runs state lotteries and organises the betting on horse races, but it is anxious that government-sponsored gambling should grow at the expense of gambling organised by petty criminals and gangsters.

Sakura

Traditional
English words translated by Edwin Markham

An alternative accompaniment could be made up by the class using just 4 notes:- F♯ G B D .
Various ostinati could be created.
Glockenspiel and Xylophone with non pitch percussion would work well.
Try to play the melody on recorders.

This is a song about the sadness of the beauty of Cherry Blossoms.
How can beauty be sad?

KANTO TELEVISION PROGRAMS

❹ NTV

5:00 Weather, :45 Report, :50 Gateball
6:15 Heart Enlightenment, :30 Religious Hour, :45 News
7:00 Tokoro's Science Variety, :30 Lure of Travel: Kagawa
8:00 Sunday Morning Show
9:30 Global Age
10:00 Sports Variety, :55 NFL '90
11:00 Trip to Japan's Masterpieces, :30 News, :45 Info Variety: Travel Club

12:55 Guide
1:00 (S) Super Jockey, :55 Guide
2:00 (S) Sunday Special: Search for the Legend of "Urashima Taro"
3:25 News, :30 Japanese Movie: Kigeki; Otoko no Komori-uta
4:55 Guide
5:00 (S) Music Variety: Otona no Manga, :15 Guide, :20 (S) Comedy Hour

6:00 (B) News, :25 Weather, :30 Sports Info
7:00 Panic TV, :30 Variety: World Adventures
8:00 Variety: Genki ga Deru TV, :54 (B) News, :57 Guide
9:00 Info Variety: Did You Know That?, :54 (B) Weather, Guide
10:00 (S) Talk Show: Oshare 30,30, :30 (B) TV Series: Remington Steele
11:26 Enterprises, :30 (B) News
12:00 Document '91, :30 All-Japan Pro Wrestling
1:25 Weather

❻ TBS

5:05 (S) Morning Pops, :15 Video Jockey, :30 (B) CBS Evening News
6:00 Golf, :30 News & Sports
7:00 Beauty Quest, :15 Cultural Topics, :30 Current Topics
8:00 In Praise of Hometowns, :30 Sunday Morning Show
9:54 Guide
10:00 Info Variety: Tokyo Magazine
11:00 Zigzag the Globe, :30 News, :40 Weather, :45 Guide, :50 Beppu-Oita Mainichi Marathon

2:24 News, :30 (S) Toray Pan-Pacific Tennis: Women's Singles, Finals
3:54 Guide
4:00 Tokyo Tug-of-War Championship, :54 Guide
5:00 Comedy Special, :30 News Forest, :50 Weather, :55 Guide

6:00 Special Report, :54 Guide
7:00 (S) Quiz: Password, :30 Variety: TV Detectives
8:00 (S) Sunday Special: World Travelogue, :54 News
9:00 Drama: Mame Hagaki, :54 Weather
10:00 (S) Wonderful Companions, :30 Kankuro Nakamura's Talk Variety
11:00 Talk Show: Ryu's Bar, :30 Sports & News
12:20 (B) CBS Documentary
1:15 (S) Amateur Band Contest

❽ FUJI

5:30 TV Museum
6:00 Drama: Wanpaku Tenshi, :30 News, :45 TV Art Museum
7:10 Art Info, :15 Current Topics, :30 Top Information
8:00 Takemura's Discussion, :30 Human Documentary
9:00 Drama: Nairu-na Totomesu, :30 Women's Talk Variety
10:00 Variety Show: Waratte Iitomo Special
11:50 (S) Fun TV, :55 News

12:00 Talk Variety, :55 Guide
1:00 Samma's Variety with Kids, :30 Sports Network
2:55 Enterprises
3:00 Horse Racing
4:00 (S) UHB Cup Ski Jump Meet (If cancelled, Variety)
5:25 Guide, :30 News: Super Time

6:00 Cartoon: Chibi Maruko-chan, :30 Cartoon: Sazae-san
7:00 Cartoon: Kiteretsu Dai-hyakka, :30 Cartoon: Trap Ikka Monogatari, :58 News
8:00 Info Quiz: Common Sense/Nonsense, :54 (B) News, Weather
9:00 Drama: Hana-sake Yonin-gumi, :54 Gourmet
10:00 Quiz: Say Quickly, :30 Shingo & Shinsuke's Talk Variety
11:00 (S) Music Fair, :30 FNN News, :45 Pro Baseball News
12:50 Horse Racing Digest
1:00 Gourmet Report, :55 Enterprises
2:00 (S) Weather

❿ TV ASAHI

6:00 Comments from Around the World, :30 News, :45 (B) CNN Morning
7:00 Fascinating Trip, :30 (S) Original Concert
8:00 Drama: Tokkyu Shirei Solbrain, :30 Cartoon: Magical Taruruto-kun
9:00 (S) Untitled Concert, :30 (S) Documentary: Japanese People in Foreign Countries
10:00 Sunday Project
11:45 Metropolitan News, :50 News

12:00 Quiz: Ceremonies, :45 Newly-weds
1:15 Panel Quiz: Attack 25, :45 (S) Popular Song House
2:55 Guide
3:00 TV Vaudeville, :55 News
4:00 All-Star Charity Golf
5:25 (S) News: 530 Station, :55 Guide

6:00 Viva! Cooking, :30 Info Variety: TV — Then & Now, :55 Weather
7:00 Global Variety: Catch Me, :30 Quiz: Hint de Pinto
8:00 Drama: Daihyo Torishimari-yaku Deka, :54 News, Weather
9:02 (B) U.S. Movie: Alien Nation
10:54 (S) See the World by Train
11:00 Night Line ANN, :30 Big Sports World
12:30 (S) What's Next, :45 (S) Club Shinsuke
1:30 (B) CNN Daywatch

⓬ TV TOKYO

5:25 Animal Families, :40 Weather, :45 Medical Science
6:00 Igo Meet, :45 (S) Business Weekly
7:00 (S) Next Wave, :30 World Big Tennis
8:00 Food & Health, :30 (S) Fishing Paradise
9:00 Current Topics with Hirotatsu Fujiwara, :30 Talk Show: 1st
10:00 News: Time Eye, :30 Golf Info
11:00 Unknown Islands of Indonesia, :55 (S) Pet Animals

12:00 Survival Golf, :25 Guide, :30 Sunday Golf
1:00 Golf Talk, :30 Ozaki's Golf
2:00 (S) Wonderful Marine, :30 World Alpine Skiing Championship Highlights
4:26 (S) Rugby: Waseda Univ. vs. Keio Univ.
5:54 Info

6:00 Evening News, :25 Weather, :30 Samurai Drama: Kurama Tengu
7:00 (S) Sunday Big Special: Children's Singing & Mimicry Grand Prix
8:54 Info
9:00 Samurai Drama: Onna Mushu-ku-nin, :54 Gourmet
10:00 (S) Enka Song Show, :30 Super Golf
11:00 Sports Today, :35 World Alpine Skiing Championship
1:30 News, :35 Motor Land
2:05 (S) Zip's, :15 Star Bowling
3:10 Horse Racing Digest

TO COPY IN YOUR TOPIC BOOK

(*filling in the blank spaces*)

1. The most popular leisure activity in Japan is.............
2. Cha no yu is the ....and Ikebana is.......... ....
3. A Noh play is a.......... .... The main character always wears a...........
4. The curtain in the Kabuki theatre is made up of..........in black, green and tan.

TO TALK ABOUT

Why do you think T.V. is so popular in Japan and also in the West? Satellite and cable television will bring many more television channels into our homes. Do you think that this will bring more interesting and entertaining programmes? Or do you think that all the new channels might be tempted to offer the same sort of programmes in order to get the biggest audiences? What do you think is the best way to pay for a television station? A licence fee? Through advertising? By paying for each programme through a meter?

TO WRITE ABOUT

Write an account of a puppet show you have seen. Explain how the puppets are worked and how they are made to speak.

TO INVESTIGATE AND DESCRIBE

Find out about the nearest theatre to where you live. What is its name? How did it get this name? Which plays are being performed at present? If you have visited it - describe what it looks like inside. Perhaps if you write to the management of the theatre and tell them about your work, they will reply with some information to help you.

TO WRITE ABOUT

What are your family's favourite sports and games? Do you like to take part or just watch? How else do you spend your free time?

TO TALK ABOUT

Traditional Japanese music often seems strange to our ears, yet the Japanese enjoy our 'classical' music. Can you think of an explanation for this? Try and listen to some Japanese music.

TO SING AND PLAY

The stamp shown on the cover of this book gives part of the Japanese Folksong - *Sakura* (Cherry Blossoms). The full melody has been written out for you on page 62 - along with a translation of the words. Try and sing and play this song in Japanese; you will find it sounds much better than the translation!

TO PREPARE AND REPORT

Conduct a survey among the class to find out how people enjoy spending their leisure time. You might make a list of 20 different leisure activities such as: Watching Television, Reading Books, Playing Soccer, Swimming etc. etc. Then you could ask your friends to put the activities in order of preference. Now you can make a graph to show your results and write a report. You might prefer to conduct your survey in a different way - if so talk to your teacher about it.

TO TALK ABOUT

Look at the T.V. Guide (page 63) taken from the *Japan Times* (a Japanese daily newspaper printed in English and bought mainly by foreigners living in Japan.) Notice the number of foreign programmes. Notice that some special stations broadcast in English. Why do you think they do this? Notice the educational channel. What sort of programmes are broadcast? Notice the number of sports programmes that are shown. Which seem to be the most popular sports?

Letters 6

Minami Junior High School,
Hiroshima City,
Hiroshima Prefecture,
Japan.

January 20th

Dear Yasmin Khan,

Thank you for your letter. I am a girl. My name is Kaoru Doi. My age is 14. There are 5 people in my family. My father, my mother, my sister and my brother, and myself. My father works for a company. I think that he is very kind and very handsome (.....?) My mother is very kind too. She made a cake yesterday. But it wasn't good. But, I ate the cake. Because I am also very kind..... (or greedy!) My brother and sister are good children but sometimes they get on my nerves. But of course I like them.

I like music very very very much. Of the Japanese singers I like 'Shonentai' and Akina Nakamori as well as others. Then I like your pop groups, too, like 'Queen' and 'A-Ha.' I also like 'The Beatles' etc. etc. I love them very much. I will go to a concert of 'Shonentai.' I hope I'll have a good time. I have many records and many tapes. I want you to listen to Japanese singers and songs. Yazzie!

My friends call me as my nick name 'Kapo' and 'Lemon' and 'Doji.' Well...I like to read books too. Sometimes I write a poem.

Then I will go to England next month....... I am only joking! I want to go to your country. I really want to go to your country. Please write to me about your country. I am waiting for your letter.

Your friend,

Kaoru Doi

Minami Junior High School,
Hiroshima City,
Hiroshima Prefecture,
Japan.

20th January

Dear Simon Bullimore,

My name is Rie Hamao. I am a girl. I am 14 years old. My eyes are black. I have black hair. So I envy you because you don't have black hair. My mother is a beautician. My father is an employee of a company. I don't have any brothers or sisters. I enjoy volleyball and sleeping. I like pop music. I will give you my picture. So will you please give me your picture. I want to see your face.

I teach some Japanese words to you.

Good Morning ....Ohayō
Hullo ....Konnichi wa
Goodbye ....Sayōnara

You will remember these words at once. I don't understand English very much. Please teach me more English.

Your true friend,

Rie Hamao

Students using a language lab for English studies at Saitama Prefectural International High School.

68

TO WRITE ABOUT

Kaoru has a collection of nick names - 'Kapo' 'Lemon' and 'Doji.' Do you have a nick name? How did you get your name? If you could change it - what would you like to be called?

TO TALK ABOUT

What can you tell about Kaoru Doi's personality from this letter? What sort of person do you think she is?

TO WRITE ABOUT

Why do you think many Japanese would envy Simon's fair hair and blue eyes? How would you like to look if you could change yourself in some way? Why is it, do you think, that so many people want to change their appearance?

TO DISCUSS

Have you remembered Rie's Japanese words? Which three words or phrases would you choose to teach a Japanese person who could speak no English? Which words would be the most useful if that person visited Britain?

Pachinko.

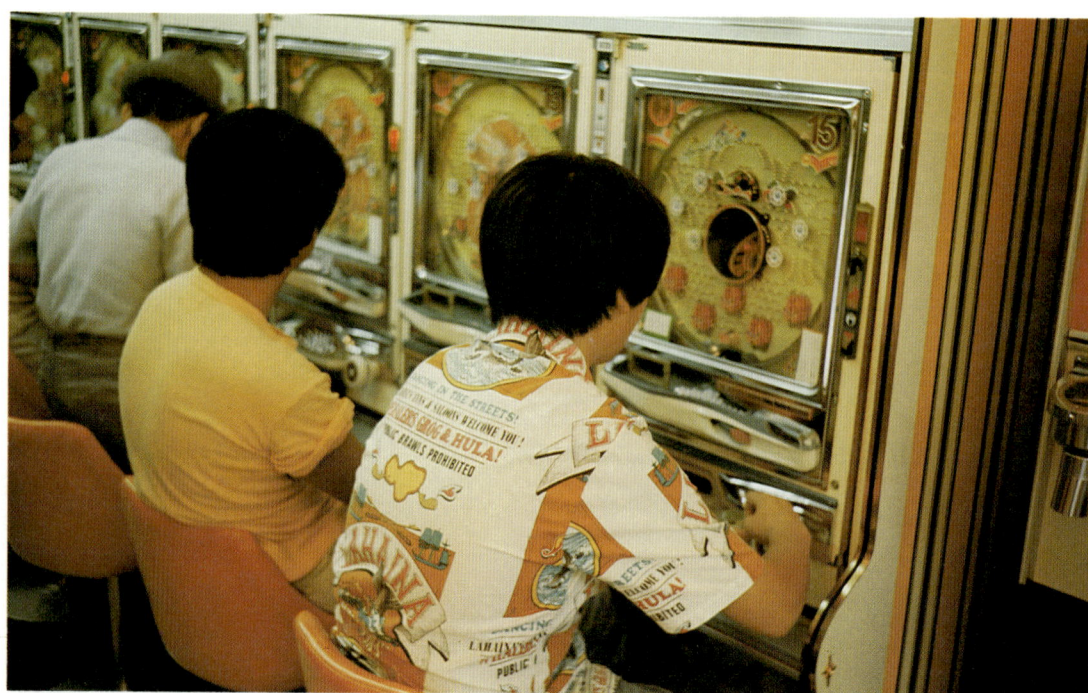

FOCUS 7:   **Language**

Some Japanese words to learn

Here you are, after you, please etc.   *dōzo*
Thank you   *arigatō*
Hello   *konnichi wa*
Goodbye   *sayōnara*
How are you?   *ogenki desu ka*
Very well thank you   *hai, genki desu*
(Girl) My name's.....   *watashi wa.....desu*
(Boy) My name's.....   *boku wa.....desu*

I'd like. Please   *.....o kudasai*
chocolate   *chokorēto*
Coca cola   *Kokakōra*
hot dog   *hotto doggu*
chips   *furenchi furai*
orange juice   *orenji jūsu*

e.g. *chokorēto o kudasai. Orenji jūsu o kudasai.*

1 *ichi*
2 *ni*
3 *san*
4 *shi* or *yon*
5 *go*
6 *roku*
7 *shichi* or *nana*
8 *hachi*
9 *ku* or *kyū*
10 *jū*
11 *jūichi*

12 *jūni*
13 *jūsan*
14 *jū-yon*
20 *nijū*
21 *nijūichi*
30 *sanjū*
31 *sanjūichi*
40 *yonjū*
50 *go jū*
90 *kyūjū*
100 *hyaku*
101 *hyaku ichi*
543 *gohyaku yonjūsan*
1,000 *sen*

Gogatsu

January	*Ichigatsu*
February	*Nigatsu*
March	*Sangatsu*
April	*Shigatsu*
May	*Gogatsu*
July	*shichigatsu*
September	*kugatsu*

TO PUZZLE OUT

What is the Japanese word for	14?
What is the Japanese for	18?
What is the Japanese for	25?
What is the Japanese for	37?
Now try these:-	62
	103
	124
	476

You have been given the Japanese for January, February, March, April, May, July and September. Now work out the Japanese for the other months.

Maru (OK)   Counting   Indicating numbers

ANSWERS:

14	=	jū-yon
18	=	jū-hachi
25	=	nijūgo
37	=	sanjūnana
62	=	rokujūni
103	=	hyakūsan
124	=	hyakunijūyon
476	=	yonhyakunanajūroku

rokugatsu
hachigatsu
jūgatsu
jūichigatsu
jūnigatsu

FOCUS 8: **Holidays**

'Japan - a Nation of Tourists'

Modern tourism in Japan may well have originated in the long pilgrimages to shrines and temples in order to worship that were common in days gone by. Today, the city shrines and temples which are usually situated in beautiful parks are still a great attraction for visitors, as are the many other historic places of Japan which attract great numbers of tourists (never without their cameras!), including parties of school children on their annual outing.

Away from the cities, some of the mountainous and coastal regions have been made into National Parks. These are areas of very great beauty. Within various parks, visitors are able to see mountains, volcanoes, hot springs, sandy beaches and coral reefs. The parks are protected from being spoilt by new buildings or industry but tourists are very well catered for. Nowadays, more and more people are travelling abroad, especially to South-East Asia, the U.S.A. and Europe, for business and pleasure

A popular skiing resort in northern Japan.

National Holidays

In Japan there are thirteen National Holidays which are like our Public (Bank) Holidays.

Holiday	Date	Celebration
New Year's Day	1 January	People eat traditional food, visit the shrine, friends and relations. It is usually a lively family celebration
Coming of Age Day	15 January	For people who have just reached their 20th birthday. They visit the shrine to give offerings of thanks for their past good fortune, and pray for a happy future
Foundation Day	11 February	To celebrate the founding of the Japanese State
Vernal Equinox	21 March	Veneration of one's ancestors
Keep Japan Green Day	29 April	'Midorinohi' A new holiday introduced in 1990 to remember Emperor Shōwa
Constitution Day	3 May	To celebrate Japan's Constitution
Childrens' Day	5 May	Also known as Boys' Festival (Day)
Respect for the Aged	15 September	
Autumn Equinox	24 September	Veneration of one's ancestors
Health Sports Day	10 October	
Culture Day	3 November	To celebrate Japan's heritage
Labour-Thanksgiving Day	23 November	
Emperor's Birthday	23 December	

If any of these holidays fall on a Sunday, then the following day is treated as the holiday. The New Year's Holiday is often lengthened. Government offices and many firms and companies close from the 29 December to the 3 of January to give their workers a week's paid holiday. The outsides of the houses are often decorated with pine and bamboo branches - and rice cakes and other special foods are eaten to bring good luck to the family.

Early in the morning of New Year's Day the family meet to wish each other 'Akemashite omedetō gozaimasu.' (A Happy New Year.) According to a long-established custom the male head of the house or the first-born son is then supposed to draw 'Wakamizu' - the first water of the year from the well or the tap. This water is placed in a bowl and all the family wash their faces with Wakamizu. Candles are then lit at the family altar and the

The summer Gion Festival in Kyōto.

first rice cakes of the day are offered to the family gods. Then, everyone drinks 'Otoso' (New Year wine) and eats 'Ozōni' (special rice cakes.) Best clothes are then put on for a visit to the shrine. Usually, the rest of the day is spent at home with the family. On New Year's Day children often play traditional games like shuttlecock and battledore. Kite flying is another favourite New Year activity.

Other Festival Days

As well as the festivals celebrated on National Holidays, Japan has very many other festivals and religious days. In fact, a festival or *matsuri* takes place somewhere in Japan on almost every day of the year. Some festivals are small - taking place in villages to celebrate such occasions as the flowering of the cherry blossoms or the rice harvest. The Kamakura or Snow House Festival is celebrated mainly in the town of Yokote in Akita Prefecture and there are other similar snow festivals in other northern parts of Japan. This festival is for children when they build a snow house for six or seven people that looks like an Eskimo igloo. A charcoal fire warms the snow house and the children heat soup and tea, and offer fruit to visitors.

Other festivals are very grand affairs, attracting many visitors and coverage on television. There are processions through the streets, people wear traditional costumes, and ancient dances and music are performed. There are many hundreds of Shintō shrines and Buddhist temples in Japan. (Shintō is the native religion of Japan.) One of the most colourful festivals is *The Gion Festival*. It takes place in July in Kyōto. This festival began during the ninth century when a plague swept through the country. The High Priest ordered that a procession of portable shrines be carried through the streets and that the people should pray that the disease would be wiped out. Nowadays, there is a procession of festival carts to remember this event. Some of these carts are as high as four-storey buildings. They have great wooden wheels. They are dragged, pushed and pulled by teams of youths through the streets of Kyōto. Some of the carts carry teams of traditional musicians. On these carts the old crafts of doll-making, weaving, dyeing, embroidery, metal work, carving and lacquer-painting are exhibited.

Boys' and Girls' Festivals

The *Girls' Festival* (Hina-Matsuri) is on 3 March and on that day the girls display the family collection of dolls. These dolls are

Above: A school visit to the Todaiji Temple, Nara, said to be the biggest wooden building in the world. *Below:* Traditional clothing is worn to celebrate Children's Day (5 May), also known as Boys' Day.

Young girls in kimono celebrate Girls Festival on 3 March with traditional doll display.

far too precious and important to play with. Japan is famous for its artistry in making beautiful dolls and most families have a fine collection of them. Usually the set contains 15 dolls. Traditionally they represent the Emperor, the Empress and all their courtiers. The dolls are dressed in fine, rich, colourful materials. Often the collections remain in the family for many years - a new doll is then only added to the set to celebrate the birth of a baby girl to the family. On Girls' Festival Day, the girls not only unpack the precious collections and display them for their friends to see - but they are also aware that the dolls they handle once belonged to their mothers, grandmothers or even great grandmothers.

The *Boys' Festival* is on 5 May. This is now officially known as Childrens' Day (*Kodomo no hi*). (Years ago a father was congratulated upon the birth of his sons, but commiserated with when his daughters were born. It was thought that boys would grow up to help him become prosperous, but that daughters would be expensive to look after and would take away much of the family's wealth when they got married. Nowadays there is a bit more equality and most fathers welcome the birth of girls and boys.)

To celebrate the childrens' festival, a bamboo or metal pole is fixed outside every house where there is a child, and a cloth streamer in the shape of a carp fish is flown from it. The streamers fill out in the wind and appear to swim in the air like real fish. (Nowadays, it is usual to fly a streamer for every member of the family. In the past only the boys counted and so it was possible to tell the number of sons in the family by counting the carp on the pole.) The carp was chosen because, by tradition, it is thought to be strong and courageous.

Holidays

Today, Japan is a very wealthy country and as a result the Japanese people are gradually making more time for leisure activities. It used to be common for employees to work every weekday and all day on Saturday. Now, most big companies have a five-day working week and paid holidays. Workers in these firms have between 100 and 120 days off per year (including weekends, National Holidays and paid holidays.)

It is quite usual for factories to organise day trips to shrines, temples and beauty spots for their employees. It has often been reported that many Japanese workers are reluctant to take the holidays to which they are entitled. They choose to work for many more hours than they have to because this strengthens their feeling of belonging to their work group who are also their best friends in many cases. However, young people do not have the same attitude to work; some think that holidays are more important to happiness and the quality of life than work.

It is usual for children to go to school on Saturday mornings and there are two main school holidays each year. The first is at New Year and the other is in the summer with a short break in March. In addition, it is usual for Japanese children in the last year at Primary School, Junior High School or Senior High School to go on a residential visit from school. These trips are called 'shūgaku-ryokō.' They usually last from three to five days. Japan's rail networks provide special trains for these outings. These trips are not holidays. They are educational visits and the children are expected to find out and record information about the places they visit.

Carp-shaped streamers (*koinobori*) are flown on Children's Day to express the hope that the new generation will be energetic and strong as the carp ascending strong rapids.

Left: The Golden Pavilion, Kyōto. *Above:* The *torii* gate of Itsukushima Shrine, on the island of Miyajima, near Hiroshima.

The whole weekend at home and paid holidays are fairly new experiences for the Japanese people. However, the popularity of family outings has increased enormously in recent years. Increased wealth has meant that more people now own cars. It is now easier for people to travel both to places of interest in the city and to tourist spots in the countryside. Although new motorways have made car travel much easier, the main roads and highways of Japan are some of the most crowded in the world. For this reason many people prefer to travel by rail and by air as it can be much quicker than on the crowded roads.

Japan's railways offer a punctual and reliable service to almost every part of the country and there is a rail-drive service for motorists. Rail travel is particularly popular in winter since it takes very little time to go from Tōkyō to the ski-resorts in the mountain regions. Also, long-distance bus companies run good services from the cities to rural areas. Public transport within the cities is good too. The very large cities like Tōkyō, Ōsaka and Nagoya have underground railways.

When they are away from home many people choose to stay in a *ryokan* or Japanese inn. These hotels are traditional in style with *tatami* mats. Visitors usually sleep Japanese-style on the floor. Futon (mattress and quilt) are kept in cupboards during the day and are only put out at night. During the day, the bedroom is used to serve meals as there is no central dining room. Food is brought to the rooms by maids. It is placed on a low table and the guests sit on the floor to eat. The *ryokan* usually has a traditional Japanese bath that is shared by all the visitors. Men and women bathe separately.

Japanese baths are much deeper than the sort that we are used to. It is the Japanese custom that you should not get into the bath until you have soaped, cleaned and thoroughly rinsed yourself from head to foot using water in a bowl outside the bath. Not before every bit of dirt and soap has been removed do you get into the bathtub where you sit together in the deep, clear, soapless, very hot water. A water heating system is kept running to make sure the water is always piping hot. After the soaking, the visitors dress in cotton kimonos (*yukata*) provided by the *ryokan*. Public bathhouses still exist in towns too but most new houses today are built with their own bathroom.

The Japanese have built many new western-style hotels. These contain single bedrooms but they are mostly used by businessmen rather than tourists. Students and young people stay in Youth Hostels. These are owned and run by local councils. They provide clean, cheap, simple accommodation for people with little money.

Ryokan.

Ofuro

Six Interesting Places for the Tourist to Visit

1. Tōkyō City

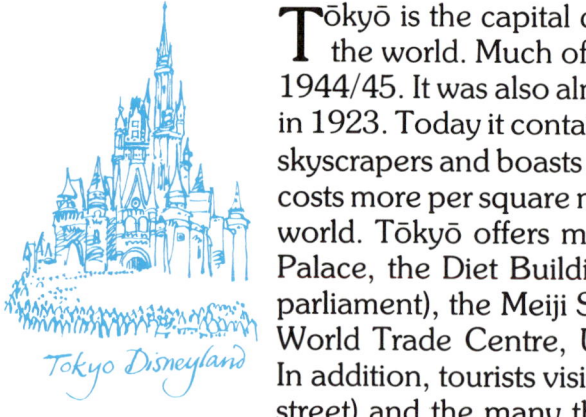

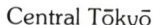
Tokyo Disneyland

Tōkyō is the capital city of Japan. It is one of the largest cities in the world. Much of Tōkyō was destroyed by fire bombs during 1944/45. It was also almost destroyed earlier by a great earthquake in 1923. Today it contains a great many modern buildings including skyscrapers and boasts a Tōkyō Disneyland. Building land in Tōkyō costs more per square metre than any other city in the industrialised world. Tōkyō offers many tourist attractions such as the Imperial Palace, the Diet Building (the Diet is the name for the Japanese parliament), the Meiji Shrine, Asakusa Temple, Tōkyō Tower, the World Trade Centre, Ueno Park, Hibiya Park and many others. In addition, tourists visit the Ginza (Tōkyō's most famous shopping street) and the many theatres, museums and restaurants.

Central Tōkyō.

2. Kyōto

This city is a former capital of Japan. It is the centre of traditional Japanese culture. Like the great cities of ancient China, Kyōto's streets were constructed in rectangular patterns. Kyōto has many shrines and temples and two old imperial castles. The city is also famous for its landscape gardens, including the famous Ryōanji temple garden which is made entirely of sand and rocks.

Mount Fuji.

3. Mount Fuji

This is the highest mountain in Japan. It is not always easy to see Mt Fuji. 'Fuji is very shy' says the tourist guide. That is another way of saying that the mountain is often hidden by clouds. It is also a mountain surrounded by superstition. It is said that visitors should not see Mount Fuji from the town of Hakone on their first visit or they will not go to heaven. At the northern foot of Mount Fuji is the Five Lake district. This is a beautiful resort area of lakes and forests popular for skating in winter and fishing in summer.

*Yomeimon Gate
Nikko*

4. Nikko and its National Park

The city is famous for the Toshogu Shrine built in 1635. It contains the tomb of Tokugawa Ieyasu, an outstanding military commander whose descendants were all-powerful for over 200 years and ruled Japan. The main building is a 5-storey elaborately-decorated pagoda. The Nikko National Park is popular for leisure pursuits - fishing, yachting, camping, climbing, skiing and skating. This area attracts thousands of visitors every year since it is only a two-hour ride by train from central Tōkyō.

5. The Seto Inland Sea - The Setonaikai National Park

This is a large expanse of water between the islands of Kyūshū, Shikoku and Honshū. It is really a chain of five seas linked together by narrow channels. The Naruto Strait is famous for giant whirlpools where the rapid current rushes into the ocean with a tremendous roar. Along the coast of the Inland Sea are many small islands, beautiful beaches and fishing villages. Now a series of bridges is being built linking Shikoku and Honshū and there are important industrial sites on reclaimed land, so the character of the Seto Inland Sea is changing.

The Seto Inland Sea.

The 'blood hell' of Beppu.

6. The town of Beppu, Kyūshū

Beppu is a spa town famous for its *jigoku* or 'hells.' These are boiling ponds - caused by volcanic activity underground - some of which eject mud into the air. 'Umijigoku' is the largest. It is the colour of the sea. The 'chinoike-jigoku' is vermilion in colour. (*Chi* means 'blood.')

7. Miyajima Island

This is one of the islands in the Seto Inland Sea. It is densely wooded with Mount Misen rising in the middle of it. On the island is the Itsukushima Shrine. At high tide the building appears to be floating since both sides of it are built over the sea. The shrine is dominated by the 'Ō-torii' - a 16-metre high red-painted wooden gateway rising out of the sea. Every Shintō shrine has a *torii* (gateway) at the entrance.

TO COPY IN YOUR TOPIC BOOK

(filling in the blank spaces)

1. In the cities, Japanese people visit..........and..........
2. In Japanese National Parks, visitors can see.........., ...,
.........., ..., ... and..........
3. Traditionally, a set of Japanese festival dolls was made up of..........dolls, an.........., ...and all their courtiers.
4. Workers in large firms have between..........and..........days off per year.
5. A Japanese inn is called a........... The bedroom floors of these hotels are covered in........... Bed covers called..........are kept in..........during the day. People have to wash thoroughly before they are allowed to get into the..........together.

TO TALK ABOUT

What do you think about the way the Japanese like to take a bath? Do you think that it is a good idea to wash before entering the bath? The Japanese think that getting in the bath while you are still dirty and then sitting in dirty water is not very hygienic. Do you like the idea of a communal bath? Although most modern homes have their own bathroom - many Japanese people still like to go to the communal bath. Is there any difference between the Japanese bath and going for a sauna?

TO CALCULATE

Compare the number of days' holiday that a Japanese worker can have, with the number of days' holiday that your father or mother has. You must include Saturdays and Sundays and all the Bank Holidays. Which country has the longest holiday?

TO DISCUSS

Some young Japanese workers are now reported as saying that they think holidays are more important to their lives than work. They refer to 'the quality of life.' What do you think they mean by that? How would you explain the difference between work and play? Is reading work? How about reading a magazine at home? Is playing football work? How about if you are a professional footballer? Is walking work? How about walking along the beach? How about going to the shop? Is swimming work?

TO PREPARE

Make a booklet describing the places in your country that you think a foreign visitor should visit. Illustrate your work.

TO RESEARCH AND REPORT

Does your country have National Parks? Find out their names and where they are. Look at the map of the National Parks of England and Wales. Are the Parks in the highland areas of the North and West, or the lowland areas of the South and East? Why do you think the National Parks are all in this region? Write to the National Park Tourist Boards for information. Are Japan's National Parks all situated in upland or lowland areas?

TO TALK ABOUT

Why do you think it was thought to be fortunate in Japan to have sons rather than daughters? In most countries where there is a king or an emperor, it is the tradition that the heir to the throne should be the eldest son - not the eldest child. In those countries a girl only inherits the throne if there are no sons. Why do you think most countries have this rule? Do you think it is a good or fair rule?

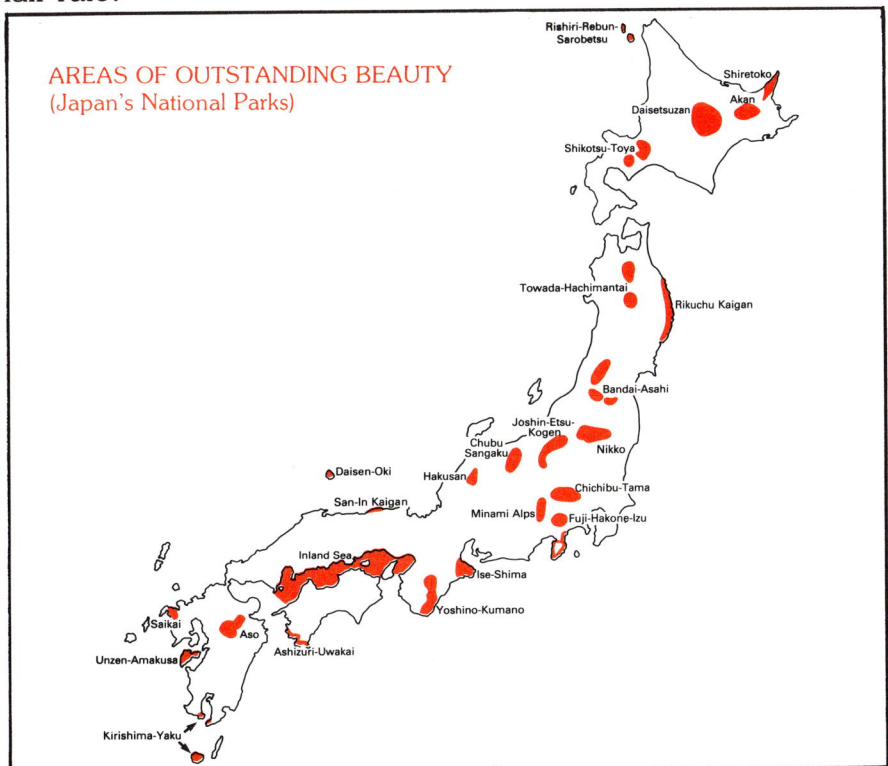

AREAS OF OUTSTANDING BEAUTY
(Japan's National Parks)

Letter 7

Minami Junior High School,
Hiroshima City,
Hiroshima Prefecture,
Japan.

January 10th

Dear Mr Colin New,

We received your students' second letters. Thank you very much. We had two weeks' winter vacation from 25 December to 7 January. We are now in the third and last semester of the school year.

We don't really celebrate Christmas but New Year's Day is the biggest day in the year to be celebrated in Japan. I will tell you how we celebrate the New Year's Day in Japan. There are many different ways to celebrate in different districts.

Mothers are very busy preparing for the day, cooking, cleaning and buying. Almost all the stores are closed for three to five days at the beginning of the year.

On the 31 December around 11.45 at night, Buddhist priests toll the bells of their temples one hundred and eight times and we pass through into the new year listening to the bells. Some people go to the Shintō Shrines after listening to the 108 bells and pray for a happy new year. Then we have a few hours' sleep. On the morning of the first, mothers serve us with some special New Year's Day dishes and special *saka* called *otoso* (a kind of herbal rice wine.)

Nengajo

Postmen deliver us New Year cards which we write around the 15 December, but the post offices keep them until 1 January. New Year's cards are special - they are coloured. We write them just like you write Christmas cards. I am enclosing the New Year card which our headmaster Mr Masaki wrote to you. As you can see there are numbers at the bottom, and this is like the numbers of a lottery. We can receive prizes.

We spend 1 January relaxing, watching television and playing some New Year's games. On 2 January we go out to visit relatives and friends. Children are given money. They buy something very special with the money, or some save the money to buy an expensive item.

I read that you have very cold weather. We have relatively warm weather. Are you and your children all right?

Very truly yours,

Satsuko Ōe

Crowds on New Year's Day at Tenmangu Shrine, Osaka.

TO TALK ABOUT

Japanese postmen work on New Year's Day - the most important holiday of the year for everyone else. Do you think it would be good if our postmen worked on Christmas Day? Would you like all your cards delivered on Christmas Day? How practical would this be for our Post Office?

TO WRITE ABOUT

Festivals are usually related to religion, so festivals around the world vary according to the different religions of the people in each country. In Satsuko Ōe's letter she tells us how the Japanese celebrate their main festival. For us our main festival could be Christmas or Eid (the Muslim festival which marks the end of Ramadan, a month of fasting) or we may have a different festival to celebrate. Explain how you celebrate your festival. What are the origins of your festival? Are there any special traditions? Are gifts exchanged? Is special food eaten?

'The polar bear was right outside the tent and it was already too late.

The polar bear wandered away in a rumbling manner - leaving only the two outer strips of the tent marked with over thirty deep slashes from its claws.'

NAOMI UEMURA

These are the words of a man only 160cm tall who climbed some of the world's highest peaks, made a 6,000km journey alone on a raft down the Amazon (eating only piranhas and bananas) and who crossed the North Pole and Greenland by dog-sled.

In 1970 Naomi Uemura was the first person in the history of mountain climbing to have topped the highest peaks in five continents.

Mt Everest   (8,848m) (Asia)   Kilimanjaro (5,895m) (Africa)
Aconcagua   (6,960m) (S. America)   Mt Blanc   (4,807m) (Europe)
Mt McKinley (6,194m) (N. America)

To mark his achievements he was given the International Award for Valour in Sport in London in 1979. Sadly, he disappeared during an attempt to climb Mt McKinley in February 1984.

His most famous adventure was crossing the North Pole and Greenland by dog-sled. Uemura prepared for these Arctic journeys for many years by living with a polar Eskimo community and making dog-sled journeys on the coastal ice. However, one night he was not prepared for the polar bear which attacked his tent. 'The temperatures were -40 to -45 and I was in my sleeping bag when I suddenly heard the dogs barking.' He realised his rifle was not loaded and so Uemura pretended to be dead. The dogs escaped and the bear ate all the seal meat and whale oil in Uemura's store. Although the bear ripped the tent, it had a full stomach and so Uemura was left unharmed. The next day he killed the polar bear when it returned to his camp. The 350-kg bear provided extra meat for the camp.

Uemura became very attached to his dogs which helped him through his loneliness and fear on this long journey. In fact, one of the huskies gave birth to nine puppies which Uemura protected from the cold with thick pelts until they were able to be taken back to base camp. Being an adventurer, Uemura was never able to rest and he was always dreaming of his next expedition.

Naomi Uemura preparing for his North Pole adventure.

BASHŌ

Another great traveller and adventurer, but one who lived 300 years before Naomi Uemura was the Japanese poet and writer Bashō. He was born near Kyōto in 1644. He set off on the first of his great journeys in 1684 and wrote about it in a book called 'The Record of a Weather-exposed Skeleton.' This first long journey took him about nine months. Travelling in seventeenth-century Japan was not easy - the roads were rough, wild and dangerous. At this time people certainly did not travel about for pleasure - it was far too risky, and usually forbidden to ordinary people.

*Bashō
on his travels*

Bashō's greatest journey was started in April 1689. Even as he planned his journey Bashō knew that it would be such a great venture, fraught with so many dangers, that he would probably not return. He even sold his house before he set out. He wrote about his journey in a diary called 'The Narrow Road to the Deep North.' For most seventeenth-century Japanese people the north of Japan was unexplored territory. It was the greatest challenge possible - it was the land of great mystery. The journey took Bashō two-and-a-half years. He returned to his home in the winter of 1691. It was a journey of about 4,000km (2,500 miles.)

This is what Bashō wrote about the start of his adventure to the North.

'It was early on the morning of March the twenty-seventh that I took to the road. There was darkness lingering in the sky, and the moon was still visible, though gradually thinning away. The faint shadow of Mount Fuji and the cherry blossoms of Ueno and Yanaka were bidding me farewell. My friends had got together the night before, and they came on the boat to keep me company for the first few miles.'

Two months later - by this time well into his journey Bashō wrote:

'I had a bath in a hot spring before I took shelter at an inn. It was a filthy place with rough straw mats spread out on an earth floor. They had to prepare my bed by the dim light of the fire, for there was not even a lamp in the whole house. A storm came upon us towards midnight, and between the noise of the thunder and leaking rain and the raids of mosquitoes and fleas, I could not get a wink of sleep. Furthermore, an attack of my old complaint made me so ill that I left the inn upon the first hint of light in the morning. I suffered severely from repeated attacks while I rode on horseback bound for the town of Kōri. It was indeed a terrible thing to be so ill on the road, when there remained thousands of miles before me, but thinking that if I were to die on my way to the extreme north it would only be the fulfilment of providence, I trod the earth as firmly as possible and arrived at the barrier gate of Ōkido.'

One of Bashō's ways of writing was to include little poems that captured his feelings during the journey. They sometimes suggest that his journey could be uncomfortable and lonely at times. He visited a temple and wrote:

'All night long
I listened to the Autumn wind
Howling on the hill
At the back of the temple.'

When he came to the site of a ruined castle and an old battlefield he wrote:

'A thicket of summer grass
Is all that remains
Of the dreams and ambitions
Of ancient warriors.'

These poems are all translations from the original Japanese. Bashō particularly liked to write *haiku*. Haiku poems are the shortest of traditional ways of writing Japanese poetry. A proper haiku should have just seventeen syllables. There should be five syllables in the first line, seven in the second line and five in the last.

One of Bashō's most famous haiku poems is about a frog

'Furuike ya,
kawazu tobikomu,
mizu no oto.'

It is translated as...

'Breaking the silence
of an ancient pond,
A frog jumped into water -
A deep resonance.'

Here is a *haiku* written in English by a poet called J. W. Hackett. It is about Sparrows in Winter and it manages the Japanese convention of 5 syllables in the first line, 7 syllables in the second and 5 in the last.

'A bitter morning:
Sparrows sitting together
Without any necks.'

Bashō was a great writer and adventurer. His way of writing travel diaries that give poetic descriptions of the places he visited and the feelings he had, have been an inspiration to many modern travel writers.

NOTE Bashō poems and text from Penguin Books *Bashō. The Narrow Road to the Deep North and Other Sketches.* Translated from the Japanese by Nobuyuki Yuasa. Published 1966.

YUKI

Another Japanese person who has struggled for success is Gunyuki Torimaru, more often known as Yuki. He thinks that if he had not had to struggle for success his work would not have been so good. Yuki produces four collections of dress designs a year, as well as being a furniture and interior designer. He says that he is not a very wealthy man, but that he would like to make enough money to improve the lives of the people who work for him.

Yuki was born and educated in Japan. After studying in England, he worked for some well-known European fashion houses, but he wanted to work for himself and become famous. At first he struggled and times were very difficult. Now he is recognised as one of the greatest fashion designers in the world.

Yuki works in his own workshop. He does not draw detailed designs - instead he prefers to work with the cloth directly on a dressmaker's dummy. He employs about twenty people to make his creations. Yuki runs his workshop in the Japanese way - he is the boss or father figure who has the responsibility of treating and caring for his workers as if they were his family. There are no strikes or disagreements - his workers will work day and night to meet a deadline - it is the aim of his employees to make the Yuki name even greater.

Yuki has said that he has no wish to design just for Japanese women - instead he prefers to make beautiful clothes for anyone in the world.

UTAMARO

Utamaro style

Kitagawa Utamaro was an eighteenth-century Japanese artist who produced pictures of the beautiful women of his time. He managed to show the charm of their faces and the smoothness of their skins. Looking at some of his pictures, you can even begin to guess about the character of some of the people he portrayed from the expressions on their faces.

Utamaro was an *ukiyoe* artist. *Ukiyoe* are pictures showing scenes from the pleasure quarters of nineteenth-century Japan where men went to forget their troubles. Many of them are woodblock prints. Utamaro had an unusual use of line and colour and many European artists like Van Gogh and Cezanne were influenced by his work. He always tried to make his pictures as simple as possible by using clear outlines. But the colours and patterns of the kimonos are highly decorative.

Drawings by Utamaro.

Some of Utamaro's critics say that all his women look the same - but if you look carefully you can see the subtle differences in the eyebrows, eyes and noses. Notice the detail in the kimonos and the great attention he paid to hair-styles.

HISAKO HIGUCHI - CHAKO

Someone else who became very famous is Hisako Higuchi - a woman golfer. She has the nickname 'Chako' - given to her by American golfers. In 1977 Chako became the first non-American golf player to win the Ladies' Professional Golf Association Championship.

At school she was excellent at athletics, particularly the 80-metre hurdles and only played a round of golf occasionally at the course where her sister worked. At the course she was spotted by an outstanding golf instructor, who realised her talent and offered to coach her. She spent hours perfecting her shots. As Chako was only 162cm tall and as she only weighed 55 kg she needed to get more power into her golf swing. Her coach decided that she should sway her waist in mid swing and that would give her the extra power she needed. This was against all the traditional golf rules but it paid off. Chako was recognised as an outstanding Japanese sportswoman.

Golf practice range

TO COPY IN YOUR TOPIC BOOK

(filling in the blank spaces)

1. Naomi..........was the first man to top the..........peaks of..........continents.
2. Yuki is a dress..........who treats his workers as his...........
3. Kitagawa..........was an eighteenth-century artist. Many European artists like..........and..........were influenced by his work.
4. Chako perfected her..........to become a great...........

TO FIND OUT AND RECORD

Find out and mark on a map of the world, the five peaks climbed by Naomi Uemura. Mark on your map the other places that he has been to on his expeditions.

TO IMAGINE, WRITE AND ILLUSTRATE

Imagine a journey by dog-sled to the North Pole. Describe three days' events in the form of a diary and make sketches to accompany your work.

TO THINK ABOUT AND DISCUSS

Travel in seventeenth-century Japan could be very dangerous. What sort of dangers do you think Bashō might have faced? What were journeys in Europe like at that time? What do you think makes an adventurer set off on a dangerous journey? Why do people climb frightening mountains or go on hazardous journeys to the Antarctic or into space? Think about the sort of adventure where before you set off, you sell your house. You know that the journey is so dangerous - you will probably not return.

TO WRITE

Haiku are short poems with a 5 - 7 - 5 syllable pattern. They are poems that try to capture the essence of a feeling or place or object. Although they always seem simple, great care has to be taken if the poems are to convey the feelings that are wanted. Try to write three haiku. One could be about a friend. Another could be about an animal - perhaps a pet. You choose the subject for your third haiku. Remember the 5 - 7 - 5 pattern. Haiku poems do not rhyme.

TO DESIGN

Yuki has asked you to design 3 outfits of your choice to include in his next collection. Perhaps one could be for evening wear to a special dance, one for casual wear and one to wear to school. Write descriptions of your outfits, suggest suitable materials and draw your creations.

TO MAKE

Fashion in Japan today is very different from that shown in Utamaro's works. Find out about traditional Japanese dress. Find out about kimonos, obi etc. Make a print copy of one of Utamaro's pictures - then design one of your own pictures. You might use lino, press print or some other way of printing. Talk to your teacher about ways of printing that might be suitable for your picture.

TO PLAN, WRITE AND DESIGN

Compare the life of Chako with an outstanding sportsperson from your country. Write about his or her life and achievements. Illustrate your work.

Contemporary and traditional (*geisha*) dress.

Letter 8

2-19-9 Kairōen,
Itsukaichi Town,
Saiki County,
Hiroshima Prefecture,
Japan 738.

O-sake

Dear Simon Bullimore,

Thank you for your letter. I received it on Monday 19 February. The date of my birthday is 19 May. I send you Japanese stamps and a photograph of me. Do you like Japanese stamps? I hope you like them. I saw a photograph of you. You are handsome. I want to see you and I want to go to England.

I was born in Hiroshima. Hiroshima is a big city. Hiroshima is famous for a Japanese wine called saké and for oyster farming. Hiroshima is also famous for the atomic bomb but Japan is on good terms with America now.

You are my first English friend and I want to be a good friend. Please be my friend for a long time.

My grandfather, Hideo, is 63 years old. My grandmother, Kumiko, is 64 years old. They live with us. My grandfather worked for a company and helped to make concrete. He is now working as a car park attendant. He likes to drink saké. One of his eyes is blue because he got something in his eye at the time of the Atom bomb in Hiroshima. He was on business at that time. My grandmother is now doing the house-keeping because my mother has a beauty shop and is busy every day.

Yours sincerely,

Rie Hamao

Letter 9

Minami Junior High School,
Hiroshima City,
Hiroshima Prefecture,
Japan.

Dear Gillian,

Thank you for your letter and for sending the many pictures. Thank you for writing my name in Japanese letters. When I saw

Yumi Fujima in Japanese I was very glad and happy. Then I showed it to everybody. Everbody said with smiles 'Waa! Oh! Oh! Oh very wonderful.'

When you had Christmas Day on 25 December you were sent many kinds of presents and I think your presents are charming. I was given a pair of pretty shoes and a three-legged stand to use to draw pictures by my father. I will answer your questions from now.

G.... What are your hobbies?

Y.... My hobbies are reading books and painting pictures. I like writing stories too. What are your hobbies Gillian?

G.... Do you have any pets?

Y.... Yes I do. My family has eight chickens and two little birds. The two female chickens are laying eggs. The eggs will be fine chicks soon.

G.... I like to play chess. Do you?

Y.... I have never played chess but I know a little about it.

G.... What kind of food do you like?

Y.... I like to eat cookies, ice cream, salad, beefsteak, sushi (a Japanese food made from raw fish and rice) and so on.

G.... Can you play a musical instrument?

Y.... I can play the piano a little. I think playing musical instruments is wonderful. I want to listen to you playing the recorder.

When I was writing this letter, my brother looked at your letter and drawings. 'Oh! I know this cartoon, it is Barbapapa' he said. He is interested in your drawings and letter.

I will tell you about my grandfather and grandmother. Grandfather and grandmother got married by a famous matchmaker forty-eight years ago. Grandmother has a dark complexion but grandfather has nice white skin. The young woman and the young man were married without ever having spoken to each other. After the wedding the bride (my grandmother) was surprised. She thought, 'How fast he talks!' Years went by and they had six children. Grandmother is very humorous and interesting to talk to. Grandfather is like her, too. He is very fit. He runs every morning. I have a great grandmother. She is 97 years old. I hope they all live for a long time.

Yours sincerely,

Yumi Fujima

Ebi (prawn)

Maguro (tuna)

Uni (sea chestnut eggs)

Tako (octopus)

Torigai (shellfish)

Hirame (flat fish)

Ika (squid)

Ikura (fish eggs)

Anago (conger eel)

O sushi

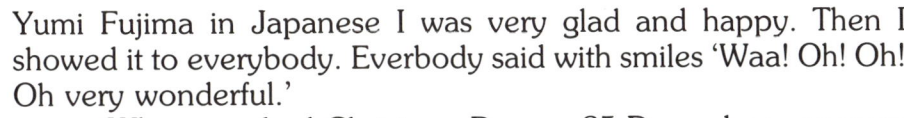

Letter 10

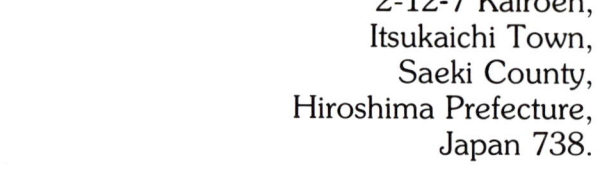

2-12-7 Kairōen,
Itsukaichi Town,
Saeki County,
Hiroshima Prefecture,
Japan 738.

Dear Rachael,

Thank you very much for your letter. I will tell you about my grandfather and my grandmother.

My grandfather was born in 1894 in Hiroshima. His name is Kunrō Terada. He lives with us. He has been sick in bed for seventeen years. He got sick because he was in Hiroshima when the A bomb was dropped. So he suffered from radio activity. He can't move besides his left hand. His condition goes from bad to worse. He was the branch manager of a bank.

My grandmother was born in 1898 in Shimane. Her name was Itsuno Terada. She doesn't live with us because she died this year. She liked flowers. She was very kind.

I will answer your question. I like music. I often listen to many records. I have many favourite pop groups. My birthday is 4 August. (I hope you like the pictures.)

Goodbye for now.

Kazue Terada

LETTER 8. TO TALK ABOUT

Why do you think that Japan is now on good terms with America. Are you surprised that these countries are now friendly after the terrible war with so much killing and suffering? Why do you think that the Japanese are particularly keen to ban Atomic warfare?

LETTER 9. TO DISCUSS

Yumi's grandparents had their marriage arranged for them by a person called a matchmaker about half a century ago. Find out about 'arranged marriages' in modern Japan. Are they as strict now as they were then? What are the advantages and disadvantages?

LETTER 10. TO TALK ABOUT

How would you reply to the very sad letter from Kazue Terada?

The principal building that survived the atomic bomb, called the Peace Dome, is preserved within the Hiroshima Peace Park.

Left: A station attendant salutes the arrival of the Shinkansen. *Above:* Policeman outside his local station.
Below: The Tokyo skyline.

FOCUS 10 **Transport**

'Rush hour lasts all day in Tōkyō!'

Moving a lot of people around is always difficult, but there are a number of things about Japan that make transport there even more of a problem than it is in most countries. Japan has the seventh largest population in the world - it has 11 cities of over a million people. It is a very mountainous country where 85% of the land is covered in mountains which means that about 80% of the people have to live on about 10% of the land space. A quarter of them live in what is called the Kantō Plain surrounding Tōkyō.

Despite all its problems, Japan has a good system of public transport. Recent years have seen major developments in air, bus and rail services.

The Railways

The history of Japanese railways goes back to the 1870s when the first steam trains went into service. The railways were taken over by the state in 1906. However, in recent years this state-run system - just like most railway systems in the western world - has cost the tax-payer a great deal of money because of its debts. In 1987 the government decided to privatise the railways into six companies looking after local services, and one company looking after a nationwide freight service.

The Japanese railway system has a complete network of safe, speedy and punctual services. Each year the railways carry more passengers than any other in the world.

Shinkansen

Of all the Japanese trains the best known are the 'Bullet Trains' on the Shinkansen. The word Shinkansen means 'the new trunk line.' The first part of this express service opened in 1964 to celebrate the Tōkyō Olympics. The railway was built on a special, smooth, jointless track so that the 16-coach trains could

Bullet train

Map of the Shinkansen route

travel safely up to speeds of 210 km per hour (130 mph.) It means that over 1,000 people can be carried in air-conditioned carriages from city to city very quickly. The southbound Shinkansen line runs from Tōkyō to Hakata, a distance of 1,069 km. The 'Bullet Trains' can travel this distance in less than seven hours linking the cities of Nagoya, Kyōto, Ōsaka, Okayama and Hiroshima. Two more recently completed lines run from Ueno station in Tōkyō to Niigata on the Japan sea coast and to Morioka in Northern Honshū.

There are two kinds of Shinkansen train - the Hikari and Kodama. The Hikari are the super express 'bullet' trains while the Kodama are slower and stop at more stations. Both kinds of train have a dining car and a buffet and a wide selection of meals and snacks can be bought. Sweets, drinks and box lunches can also be bought from the sales staff who continually go from carriage to carriage pushing trolleys of refreshments. The super-express trains include compartments for wheel-chair passengers and it is also possible to make telephone calls from the trains. All Shinkansen trains have a radio telephone service which links the train to most big cities. The service is mostly used by businessmen. One problem with Shinkansen trains is the lack of baggage space. Passengers are encouraged to travel with as little luggage as possible so as not to hold up trains in stations or block the gangways. Some passengers send their heavy luggage on ahead.

When you reserve a seat on the train you know which carriage you will be sitting in. It is not necessary to go chasing down the platform looking for the carriage when the train arrives because the train is designed to pull up alongside the platform with the carriages and doors always in the same place. The points are marked on the platform and passengers queue up beside the mark shown on their ticket. 'Green Cars' are First Class carriages.

The Shinkansen system has a wonderful safety record. A great many safety measures have been built into the system. There are electronic monitors of every sort installed along the track. There

Winter farmland scene in the Mount Aso region, Kyūshū. The Shinkansen lines goes to Kyūshū as far as Fukuoka.

are monitors to warn of floods, strong winds, blocked lines and, most important of all, of earthquakes. Japan has on average about 10 earthquakes a day. Fortunately, most of these are very small - too small for most people to even notice. Sometimes, however, the earthquakes are much stronger and it is believed that one day Japan will suffer another huge earthquake like the one in 1923 which killed over 100,000 people and destroyed two-thirds of Tōkyō. If a monitor along the track picks up a severe earthquake signal the electric current is automatically shut off and the trains in the area stop.

While the Shinkansen has brought a well-organised, punctual, high-speed train service to Japan, it has also brought its share of problems. Japanese people often complain that it is a system that is too costly to build and maintain. They also complain that it is too noisy. Although the passengers travel in soundproofed carriages at 200 km per hour, the vibration and roar of the train is unbearable to those living anywhere near the railway tracks. The trains also bring thousands of visitors to Tōkyō each day, making an already crowded city even busier.

Subway train.

Local and Subway Trains

Travelling on the local and subway trains is by no means as comfortable as Shinkansen travel. Like the London underground trains passengers are allowed to stand which means the carriages are often very crowded.

Six cities in Japan have subway trains: Tōkyō, Ōsaka, Nagoya, Sapporo, Yokohama and Sendai. The underground trains are the fastest means of transport in and around the big cities and carry most of the people who go to work.

"Pushers"

Some people say the 'rush hour' on Tōkyō's expressways lasts all day!

Rush hour in Japan lasts from 7.30 - 10.00 a.m. in the morning and from 4.30 - 7.30 in the evening. Most stations employ extra staff during these hours to help pack people into train carriages by pushing in those people who are still partly hanging out of the doorways. Carriages with seats for 70 people often carry 350 people during rush hour.

Road Transport

Japan's express railway system is today so efficient that most people prefer to travel long distances by train. However, the additional motorways are encouraging more people to use their cars. City roads in Japan are very crowded indeed. During the rush-hour period cars and lorries can only creep along very slowly. (The Japanese call rush hour 'Rasshuawā'.) Sometimes all the traffic just seems to stop. The average speed in Tōkyō, for example, is around 8 mph.

In some parts of Tōkyō people are not allowed to use a car unless they can show a police certificate saying that they have their own off-street parking space. Parking in Tōkyō is very difficult and very expensive. Many Tōkyō car owners cannot afford to drive to work in the city each day because they cannot afford the car-parking charges.

For these reasons most people travel to work by bus or subway train. Some people even go by taxi. They are usually painted in bright colours and have a coloured roof lamp. Taxi doors are automatic - passengers are unable to open the door of a taxi to get in or out, nor can they close the door after they are allowed out. Doors are controlled by the taxi driver from his seat. Being in a taxi in Japan can be a nerve-racking experience. Some drivers are particularly scary: they rush from space to space and from lane to lane in an attempt to force a way through the crowds of traffic on some of the busiest roads in the world.

Shipping

Japan has the world's second largest merchant fleet (Liberia has the largest.) Even so, one half of Japan's imports are carried to her shores by foreign ships. She also has an enormous number of small coastal vessels which link the hundreds of harbours all round the coast.

Airlines

As in all countries, airlines have grown a great deal in recent years. Japan's original international airline, which is now privately owned, is Japan Air Lines (JAL). In addition, there is Japan's biggest domestic airline, All Nippon Airways (ANA), which

Port Island, Kobe.

today is also a major international carrier. Both airlines continue to provide domestic flights together with a third airline called Japan Air System. Typical routes are Tōkyō - Sapporo 1hr 25mins; Tōkyō - Hiroshima 1hr 30mins; Tōkyō - Aomori 1 hr 10mins. In Tōkyō these domestic flights leave mostly from Haneda Airport. There is a monorail link from the airport to the city centre. International flights in Tōkyō use Narita Airport. It is over 60 km from the city centre. There have been many arguments about Narita Airport. Some people were very angry that good farm land was taken to build the airport. Other people complained that an airport 60 km from the city centre was too far. They said that it added to the strain of a long journey for passengers arriving in Japan from other parts of the world.

Narita International Airport.

TO COPY IN YOUR TOPIC BOOK

(filling in the blank spaces)

1. Japan has the..........largest population in the world. It has 11 cities of over a..........people.
2. Japan's super express train system is called.......... The 16-coach trains manage speeds of up to..........per hour.
3. Hikari are the.......... ....trains.
4. Six major cities have subway trains. They are.........., ..., ..., ..., ... and...........

TO TALK ABOUT

Why do you think that the Japanese people fear a major earthquake between 7.30 - 10.00 a.m. and 4.30 - 7.30 p.m. more than at any other time? Imagine that you lived in a country where a major earthquake was possible at any time. Would this affect the way you lived?

TO PLAN AND DESIGN

If you were making a television advertisement about the Shinkansen trains, what advantages of the train service would you show? Write a script with pictures of your planned commercial. You might be able to turn it into a short play.

TO TALK ABOUT

In 1987 the Japanese government decided to privatise the railway network because it was not making a profit; instead it was costing the tax-payers too much money! Do you think that a cheap public transport system should be paid for by the government from taxes, in an attempt to reduce the number of cars on the road? Or do you think that it is unfair for car owners to have to pay for other people's cheap rail and bus fares?

TO INVESTIGATE AND REPORT

What do you know of your own country's railway system? How does the system compare with regard to speed, safety, efficiency, service etc.? How are you going to get the information you require? Report your findings in a booklet called 'Our Railway.'

TO DISCUSS

Do you think it is a good idea that in Tōkyō people should have their own parking space before they are allowed to buy a car? Do you think that city councils in our country should make a law like this? Is it unfair that only people with their own parking spaces should be allowed to own cars?

FOCUS 11   **Food**

'Let's open our stomachs and talk'

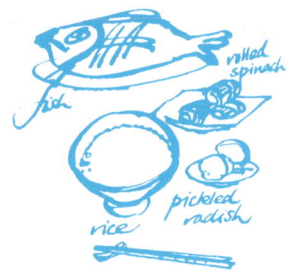

'In Japanese the word for food and the word for rice is the same'

'When I first went to Britain many years ago, I was shocked to find English cooking so plain. The roast beef and mutton to me were rather tasteless, their boiled cabbage was very watery, and their "sweets" were not particularly palatable. However, after spending several years there, I developed a great liking for English food, which is of course very wholesome.'

This is what Ichirō Kawasaki wrote about English cooking in his book *The Japanese are Like That*. It is interesting to see that he found English food plain and tasteless. Perhaps we would find a lot of Japanese food strange at first and again we might describe some of it as 'tasteless.' The food that the people of a country eat usually depends upon the foods that are easily available. The way that these foods are served is usually the result of hundreds of years of experimentation. A country's climate and the needs of its people also help to decide the sort of foods that are eaten and the way they are served.

What, then, are the foods of Japan that we would find strange and tasteless? The Japanese diet is mainly made up of three ingredients: fish, rice and vegetables.

A Japanese breakfast.

Fish

It is easy to see why fish was used by the Japanese as one of their main foods. It is still their main source of protein. Most of Japan is so mountainous that it is impossible to use it as farming land either for growing crops or for raising animals. As Japan has so many people to feed and so little flat land, she is largely dependent on the sea for food.

The Japanese eat raw fish but they are very careful in the way they choose which raw fish to eat. The fish have to be very fresh and only certain types are suitable for eating raw. Other types would cause terrible food poisoning. Raw fish comes in two main ways - either as *sashimi* or *sushi*.

Sashimi is sliced raw fish served on a plate with a little grated radish. It is eaten after dipping into a small saucer of soy sauce and radish. *Sashimi* is usually served along with other foods or as the first part of a much bigger meal. A mild radish called *daikon* is used.

Sushi, however, is usually served as a meal in itself. Many people say this is the finest meal from Japan. It is made up of raw fish, rice and vinegar. A *sushi* restaurant always has a long counter. On top of the counter is a glass showcase in which the raw fish of the day are on display. The *sushi* chef expertly slices the fish chosen by the customer - rolls a ball of vinegar and rice, puts a dash of strong green mustard on the rice ball, and then lays the sliced fish on top. The *sushi* is lifted up in the fingers, dipped in a bowl of soy sauce and popped into the mouth in one go with a slice of red ginger called *shōga*. The most popular *sushi* is that made from *maguro*, tuna fish. The *sushi* chef continues to prepare mouth-size portions until the customer is full.

Sushi.

A-ji-ta-ta-ki
~ raw pompano fish
served on radish,
seaweed & hojiso
flowers

Fugu is another well-known but rare fish dish. *Fugu* is the globe fish. Great care has to be taken in preparing the meal as parts of the fish are deadly poisonous. *Fugu* restaurants must get a special licence from the government to show that the owners know the proper way to serve the fish. A few years ago a famous Japanese actor died after eating *fugu*. Perhaps knowing that one is eating a poisonous fish adds excitement to the meal!

As well as eating it raw - the Japanese also enjoy fish which has been cooked. Fish is cooked in many ways. For the Japanese fish has the same importance that meat has in a western diet. Every day a large part of the catch from Japan's huge fishing fleet is sold in Tōkyō. This fleet fishes in all the oceans of the world. The variety of fish on sale in Japan is probably greater than anywhere else.

Japan's yearly catch of fish is the biggest in the world. Hundreds of different sea foods are eaten - fresh, dried, smoked and pickled. Shark's fins, *katsuobushi* (dried, boned, flaked fish used for soup making), oysters, dried squid, boiled octopus, eels and shrimps (sometimes made into sausages) are all enjoyed by the Japanese. Often very small fish are eaten including their bones. In this case not only does the fish provide protein but also some of the minerals needed by the body.

So important is fish to the Japanese that the country has led the world in discovering and inventing new fishing methods. Sea farming, making enormous artificial breeding grounds and using electronic equipment to find shoals of fish, have made Japan the great harvester of the sea.

Eating rice with chopsticks.

Sukiyaki: sliced beef with vegetables cooked at the table.

For a country so dependent on fish it is perhaps surprising that some parts of the Japanese coastline can no longer be fished because the waters have been poisoned by chemical and industrial wastes from factories inland. Japan is now very concerned about this sort of pollution and is trying to prevent any further pollution of its waters.

Because the waters around Japan cannot provide all the fish she needs, her fleets have to travel the world. Indeed, sometimes Japan has been accused of being too greedy and of over-fishing the world's oceans. Experts say that the supply of fish for the world must be shared. They stress that it must be protected if people are to continue to get fish from the sea. Some types of fish are dying out because of over-fishing.

Many people are especially critical of Japan's whaling industry. They say that the widespread hunting of whales especially by Japan has already put some species at risk of extinction and that other species are severely at risk. The Japanese claim that most of their whale hunting is now strictly limited and is only carried out for scientific research. This claim is rejected by many conservationists.

Another harvest from the sea that is important for the Japanese is sea-weed. One kind which is widely used is called *kombu*. *Kombu* grows in the shallow waters in the north and it is used for making soup and as a vegetable in other dishes.

Seaweed for black hair

Shabu-shabu. Thinly sliced beef and vegetables cooked in boiling water.

Sashimi (raw fish).

Rice

In Japanese the word for food and the word for rice is the same (*gohan*). Like potatoes, rice is very productive, and in Japan it is grown on over half the farming land. Sometimes people in western countries find it difficult to understand that most Japanese prefer rice to bread and potatoes. It is true that the Japanese countryside and climate make the growing of wheat very difficult,

Sun flag lunch

but it must also be said that they do not think of rice as a poor alternative to other foods. Given the choice of rice, bread or potatoes - the vast majority of Japanese people would choose rice. However, more and more young people in Japan are eating western-style 'fast foods' like hamburgers as often as they can. As a result, the demand for rice has been going down very slightly each year. Even so, most Japanese adults will insist on having at least one bowl of rice a day. Ichirō Kawasaki says 'The Japanese love of rice is deep. They do not believe that any meal is really substantial without rice.'

A popular Japanese lunch is called the 'Sunflag' lunch. This is made up of a small tin full of boiled rice - it has no other food except a red pickled plum buried in the centre. People have said that it reminds them of the Japanese flag with its round red sun on a white ground.

Considering that only a very small amount of land is suitable for growing crops, it is a great achievement that all the rice that is needed is grown within Japan. One reason for the success has been efficient farming methods. Good fertilisers and specially designed machines are used on the small farms. Most of the farms are as small as 2½ acres. In many cases farm-workers are now women or old people - the younger men usually work in the cities during the week but help out on the farm at the weekends. Another help to rice production has been the use of a new rice grain specially developed to grow in cold climates. This has been used very successfully in the northern island of Hokkaidō. Japan now produces more rice than it needs.

Rice paddy and farmhouse.

Rice cooker

The main reason for the continued success of the rice harvest has been the Japanese government's much-discussed policy of paying a bonus to farmers who grow rice. After the rice harvest each year, the government pays the farmer a price for the grain that has been produced. This is a price that is high enough to satisfy the farmers. The government then fixes a lower price for the sale of rice to the Japanese housewife. Some critics of this system say that the price of rice is still kept too high. They say that it would be much cheaper to import rice from other countries. The government will not allow this to happen because it believes that Japan should not be too dependent on other countries for its staple food supply. Besides, the Japanese prefer the taste of Japanese-grown rice.

The preparation of rice for the family meals (it is usually eaten with breakfast, lunch and evening meal) meant that traditionally the Japanese housewife had to spend hours every day carefully boiling rice over a charcoal brazier. However, in 1955 an electric rice cooker was invented. This became widely available in the shops and it is said that this, more than anything else, has changed the Japanese woman's way of life. At the flick of a switch perfect rice can now be produced for the family. With automatic clocks - even the switching on needs no supervision. The Japanese woman's freedom from the daily chore of rice cooking, along with all the other labour-saving gadgets now available, has meant that other things can now be done with the spare time. More and more women go out to work. Others join clubs and day schools to practise their hobbies. Many others have become very actively involved in the school life of their children. As well as supervising their childrens' hours of homework, most mothers are very active members of local parent-teacher organisations.

Vegetables

As well as rice, wheat and barley are also grown in Japan, but the amounts are tiny in comparison with the quantity bought from abroad. (Tea has always been an important crop). Other fruit and vegetables that are grown include potatoes, soy beans, aubergines, cabbages, onions, radishes, mushrooms, mandarin oranges, tomatoes, apples, pineapples, grapes, pears, peaches, tobacco and sugar beet.

Noodles of various sorts are very popular. *Soba* is a thin brown or dark green noodle made from buck wheat flour, while *udon*

Some Japanese vegetables

Cha Soba

Chikara Udon

Hiya mugi

and *sōmen* are white and made from either wheat or corn flour. These noodles look a bit like spaghetti. In Japan it is good manners to make slurping noises (but not too noisily!) when eating soup or noodles.

Insutanto rāmen are plastic cups full of dried noodles - this was the first instant Japanese meal. The dried noodles, soy sauce and vegetables need only hot water to convert them into a snack and often vending machines provide the hot water too. Cup noodles are very popular with workers who do not want to use their time sitting over a meal at lunch time. Many workers want a quick, cheap, hot meal which is easy to prepare. Cup noodles can now be bought in many other countries of the world. Most brands are made under licence from a Japanese company.

Food and Health

On working days the Japanese do not spend a long time over their meals. If the rice cooker has given Japanese women more free time - modern life does not seem to have given much free time to the men. Many workers take up to two hours travelling to work each day and many companies expect their workers to work late into the evening. Even then, frequently the men do not go straight home from work, but spend a couple of hours with their workmates in bars or clubs before going home.

Considering the small amount of time that is spent eating together, it is strange that the Japanese should speak of *hara*. *Hara* is the stomach and it is believed to be the centre of feelings and emotions. (The Japanese talk of *hara* in the same way that we talk of the heart.) When someone says *Hara o watte hanashimashō* it means 'Let's open our stomachs and talk.' It is often said in Japan that words are not needed for feelings to be shared - but that people can talk from stomach to stomach. The connection of stomach and emotions in these ideas, seems to be as far-fetched as our odd connection of romance and the heart.

The number one killer in western countries is heart disease. People often think that it is cancer, but that is not so. Heart disease is the main killer in all industrialised countries except Japan. For some reason the Japanese do not seem to get as much heart disease as Europeans and Americans. (In Japan 14% of deaths are caused by heart disease - in Britain it is 48%.)

A study of Japanese people who were living in Hawaii and

California was carried out by an American called Dr Kagan. He discovered that the Japanese who had adopted an American life-style and eating habits were suffering from just as much heart disease as the Americans. He found that those living in Hawaii - where the life-style and eating habits were a mixture of the American and Japanese ways of life, had a higher risk of heart attack than native Japanese - but their risk was less than the Americans. Dr Kagan suggested that the reason for this was the Japanese diet of fish, rice and vegetables. Many doctors believe that eating animal fats is a factor towards heart disease. As we have seen there are very few animal fats in the Japanese diet.

About 40% of our food comes directly from animals while the percentage in Japan is only 20%. Even so, this 20% is 4 times as much as it was 30 years ago. Perhaps this is one reason for the steady increase in Japanese heart disease too. However, it should also be noted that the height and weight of young people have also increased. The average height of a 17-year-old Japanese teenager is now 7 centimetres more than it was before 1939. Average weight has also increased by 5½ kilograms in this time. Some Japanese are overweight. At one time it was thought that a fat Japanese was a rich Japanese. Now people realise that being overweight can cause ill health.

It is known that cigarette smoking is the cause of many deaths in Japan. About 60% of men still smoke. This is a much higher percentage than in most developed countries, although the percentage is gradually declining.

Presenting Food

Food showcase

Although everyday eating is usually a rather hurried process, Japanese foods are almost always arranged so that they are good to look at as well as good to eat. The Japanese believe that the appetite is encouraged by colour and so food is arranged on bowls and plates specially chosen for their shape and colour. Almost all Japanese soups are clear - this allows the eater to admire the pieces of delicately shaped vegetables, as well as the decoration at the bottom of the soup bowl.

Many restaurants have the custom of putting displays of the main dishes with their prices in a showcase so that it is easy to know what is on the menu. These displays are made of plastic - many are so realistic that it can be rather strange to see shop assistants dusting the plastic 'food' in the shop window!

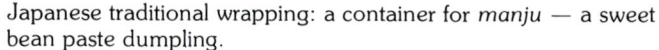

Japanese traditional wrapping: a container for *manju* — a sweet bean paste dumpling.

A restaurant's 'plastic' display of its choice of dishes.

Packaging

As well as the food on the plate being attractively presented - the Japanese also have the custom of taking great care with the way they package items for their customers. Nowhere is the Japanese art of packaging seen to greater advantage than in the traditional ways still sometimes used to pack food. In country districts, straw holders are occasionally used to pack eggs. Eggs are fragile and need protection and with rice as the main crop it was easy and sensible for the farmers to wrap their eggs in rice straw.

Chopsticks

Chopsticks

The Japanese, like the Chinese, use chopsticks for eating. To people who do not know how to use them they feel awkward and clumsy, but when used by a Japanese person they are precise and efficient. As eating habits change and steak and chips become popular - so there is a change in eating tools. Most Japanese homes now have knives and forks as well as chopsticks. When eating western foods, knives and forks are usually used, whereas chopsticks are used for traditional Japanese food.

New Habits

Meron Jusu
MELON JUICE

Kora Furoto
COLA FLOAT

It is true that the Japanese are changing their eating habits. Many Japanese people, especially the young and the middle-aged, breakfast on jam, buttered toast and instant coffee. Many people now drink beer rather than saké (rice wine) but this is usually a Japanese product. Whisky is also popular. Of the Japanese brands, Suntory Japanese Whisky is the most famous. Bread, meat and dairy products are all very expensive in Japan. Green tea is the usual drink and is served with every meal.

To a western person a traditional Japanese breakfast can be a very difficult meal. To be faced first thing in the morning with a bowl of fish soup, a bowl of rice and a raw egg, a block of bean curd along with a dish of green tea, causes for most westerners, a quick loss of appetite. For most non-Japanese the traditional breakfast is an impossible meal to enjoy (at least at first). Perhaps most Japanese react in the same way to the traditional English breakfast of fried eggs, bacon, fried bread, buttered toast, marmalade and a cup of milky tea.

Special Meals

Suki Yaki

The two meals that westerners seem to enjoy more than any others are *sukiyaki* and *tempura*. Neither of these is really a traditional Japanese meal at all. *Tempura* may have come from the Portuguese and *sukiyaki* is perhaps an adaptation of Chinese cooking.

Tempura is best eaten at the chef's counter. Fresh fish, shell fish and fresh vegetables are dipped in a very light batter of flour and egg and quickly deep-fried in vegetable oil. The chef picks out the cooked pieces and serves them in front of the customers. The pieces are picked up with chopsticks, dipped into soy sauce mixed with white radish and then eaten while still piping hot. The chef continues preparing *tempura* so that the customer has a continual supply to choose from.

Sukiyaki is cooked on the dining table in an iron pot with a gas burner beneath. The guests sit round and take what they wish from the cooking pot with their chopsticks. The main ingredients are thin slices of beef, mixed chopped vegetables, and bean curd. A small bowl containing a raw egg is given to each guest and the food is dipped into this before eating. Bowls of rice are served with the meal.

TO COPY IN YOUR TOPIC BOOK

(filling in the blank spaces)

1. Ichirō Kawasaki said: 'When I first went to the British Isles I was shocked to find English cooking so.........., their roast beef and mutton were rather.........., their boiled cabbage was very..........and their "sweets" were not particularly...........'
2. The Japanese diet is mainly made up of.........., ...and.........
3. As well as eating it raw the Japanese also enjoy..........which has been cooked. Indeed..........is cooked in many ways for the Japanese.
4. In Japanese the word for food and the word for..........is the same. Rice produces more..........per square metre than any other crop except potatoes and is grown on over..........the farming land.
5. *Insutanto rāmen* are plastic cups full of dried...........

TO DISCUSS

What are the advantages and disadvantages of the Japanese diet? What are your favourite foods and why?

TO TALK ABOUT

Why do you think there are so few sheep and cattle farms in Japan?

TO WRITE ABOUT

If you decided to give up eating animal fats, which foods would you miss the most? Do you think you could be fit, healthy and content - eating the same sort of foods as the Japanese?

TO DISCUSS

Why do you think that the Japanese should be particularly bothered about the pollution of the sea? What sort of things can poison or kill marine life? If the governments of the world were to get together to stop people from using the sea as a dump for their rubbish - what sort of laws would be needed? How could the oceans of the world be policed? How would these laws be enforced?

TO INVESTIGATE AND REPORT

Find out from reference books all you can about the growing of rice. Produce a stage-by-stage set of instructions with illustrations for a farmer who has never grown rice before.

TO TALK ABOUT

What do you think about the Japanese Government's policy of paying their farmers to produce rice that could be bought cheaper from other countries? Do you think this is a sensible idea?

TO PLAN

Plan a day's meals for you and your family that include no animal fats at all. Compare this with your favourite breakfast, lunch and tea.

A *tempura* (deep fried fish and vegetables) restaurant.

Letter 11

Kumiko Takebe,
3-12-8 201 Narashinodai,
Funabashi City,
Chiba Prefecture,
Japan.

20th January

Dear John,

Please excuse me for not having answered your letter sooner. I'm very sorry to have put off writing my answer to you till today, though I've been thinking of it.

Will you please teach me your address John? Then my next letter will go to your home. Is that all right?

Meanwhile, on the other hand, you asked about Mitsukoshi. You say your teacher has told you about the big Tōkyō store on the Ginza. Your teacher told you about the Mitsukoshi shrine.

the Ginza

In fact, as you said, in Mitsukoshi, there is a roof-garden in which we can see a kind of Shintō Shrine to worship. Oinarisan, the God of Harvest, is worshipped there. Belief of God of the Harvest has been expanded into belief of every profit. Perhaps, in Mitsukoshi, they worship the shrine hoping for the success and development of their Company. I am told that the officers of Mitsukoshi Department Store pray every morning, clapping their hands twice regularly. (Praying with claps is one of the Japanese traditional customs.)

You asked if the shop assistants had to do exercises each morning before the start of work. Many companies have this habit.

Next I'll tell you about my school life. Next Saturday is a marathon, a mass meeting. How unlucky! Send for assistance. I become a ninth grade next year. I don't want to become a ninth grade. We must take an entrance examination next year.

Next I'll tell you about some lessons. English lesson is a very good time. What subjects do you like best? In history we learned about your country.' It was enjoyable.

If you have any pictures of yourself at hand please let me have one. I'll send you mine if you want it. I have written a short letter today but I'm going to write a long one next time.

Please write to me soon this time, not making me wait as long as before. Of course I'll do the same.

Now goodbye,

Kumiko

TO TALK ABOUT

Mitsukoshi on Tōkyō's busiest street - The Ginza - is a very famous department store. It is visited by thousands of shoppers every day - rather like Harrods and Selfridges in London. Kumiko explains that the store has a Shintō shrine where the workers can pray for the success of the Mitsukoshi company. What do you think about this idea?

TO DISCUSS

It is the custom in many companies - not just shops - to start the day with organised physical exercises. Workers gather together to bend and stretch and jump etc. to music - so that they will be fit and ready for the day's work. Would you be surprised to look through the shop windows of Marks and Spencers or Woolworths to see all the shop assistants exercising in this way before opening the shop for the day? Do you think it is a good idea? Would it make the workers any better at their job?

TO TALK ABOUT

Kumiko refers to 'a marathon, a mass meeting.' She does not seem to be looking forward to it. Japanese children spend hours, especially after school, training for sports events and team matches. Do you think more time should be spent on sport in your school?

Department store.

FOCUS 12   **More Facts**

Did you know...?

Ni~sun

Hon~Source

The Japanese call their country *Nippon* - this means the source of the sun so you can see why it is often called the 'Land of the Rising Sun.' The flag has a red sun on a white ground.

Japan is a country made up of many islands. The four main islands are Hokkaidō, Honshū, Shikoku and Kyūshū and if you look at your map you can see that they are arranged rather like the shape of a boomerang. Japan also has over 3,000 smaller islands. (Some of these islands are large enough to support large villages on them while others are just tiny rocks.)

Japan has a long rocky coastline. No point in Japan is more than 150 kilometres from the sea.

Japan has great natural beauty. About 85% of its land is mountainous and this is mostly covered in forest. This means that Japan's people, agriculture and industry have to make do with only 15% of the total land area. Mount Fuji is Japan's most famous mountain - it is also the tallest with a height of 3,776 metres. Mt Cook in New Zealand South Island is about the same height at 3,764 metres. Mt Kosciuska in the Australian Alps is 2,230 metres, and Ben Nevis, Scotland's tallest mountain, is 1,347 metres.

Japan's rivers tend to be short, swift and steep. This means that they are not really suitable for river traffic but they do provide water to use on the farm land and opportunities for the development of hydro-electric power. The largest fresh water lake in Japan is Lake Biwa near Kyōto. (There is a legend that a baby girl washed in the water of Lake Biwa will grow into a most beautiful woman. Perhaps this is why the most beautiful Japanese women are said to come from the Kyōto area.)

Road transport across Japan's mountainous countryside is frequently difficult. It is often easier to travel by sea or air. Many coastal vessels connect the dozens of little ports that can be found all round the coast.

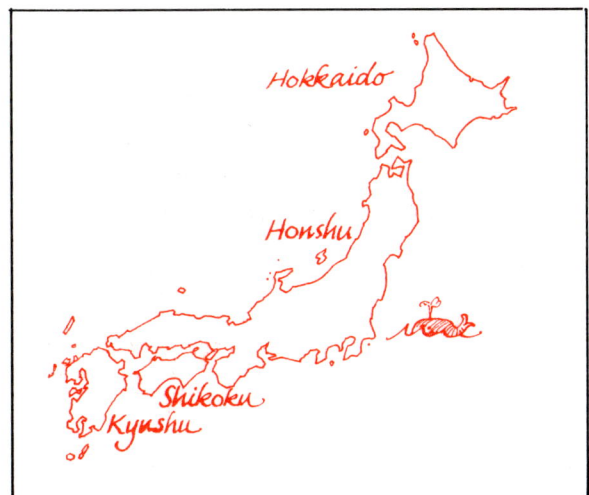

Hokkaido

Honshu

Shikoku

Kyushu

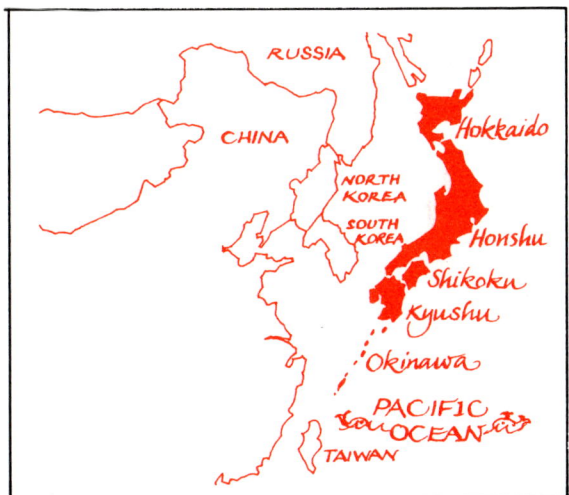

RUSSIA

CHINA

NORTH KOREA

SOUTH KOREA

Hokkaido

Honshu

Shikoku

Kyushu

Okinawa

PACIFIC OCEAN

TAIWAN

Central Japan

Biwako
Ukimido Temple

Fishing village

Mount Fuji
and
Cherry blossom

Japan's neighbours are the U.S.S.R., North and South Korea and China. The largest island is Honshū. It is about the same size as England, Scotland and Wales. The northern island of Hokkaidō is a little smaller than Wales. The journey to South Korea by boat takes 15½ hours. Most Japanese prefer to fly when they go abroad.

Flying to Japan

Tōkyō can be reached from Britain by flying the 'Silk Route' via Paris, Rome, Athens, Teheran, New Delhi and Bangkok - this journey takes about 27 hours by modern jet. It can also be reached by flying the 'Polar Route' via Anchorage, Alaska (18 hours) or via Moscow on the 'Trans-Siberian Route' (15 hours.) There is now a direct (non-stop) route from London via Siberia which takes 12 hours. From Australia Japan can be reached from Sydney in about 9½ hours or from Perth in about 10 hours.

Population

As you know, Tōkyō is the capital of Japan. It has a population of 11) million people. This makes it the second largest city in the world. (Shanghai is the largest and it is thought that Mexico City will soon overtake Tōkyō.) London has a population of 7 million. Sydney has a population of 3 million.

There are 123 million Japanese people. (Britain has a population of 56 million.) Japan now has the sixth largest population in the world. (Only China, India, the U.S.S.R., the U.S.A. and Indonesia have more people.) Although Japan has a very large population it is certainly not a large country in area and this is what makes it one of the most crowded nations in the world. In Japan there are 306 people per sq. km. compared with 229 people per sq. km. in Great Britain and just 2 people per sq. km. in Australia. In Japan nearly three-quarters of the people live in cities - most live in the four areas in and around Tōkyō, Ōsaka, Nagoya and Kitakyūshū. Japan is so mountainous that the cities are crowded together on the small amount of flat land along the coasts. According to the Japanese government, the population will grow to 140 million people by the year 2050.

Stone Age people settled in Japan many thousands of years B.C. It is thought that they came from Siberia, China, Korea and from the islands of the South Pacific. Since about the seventh

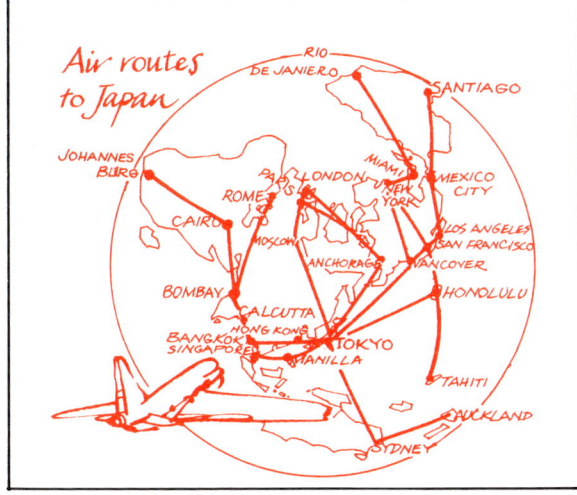

Air routes to Japan

Downtown Tokyo

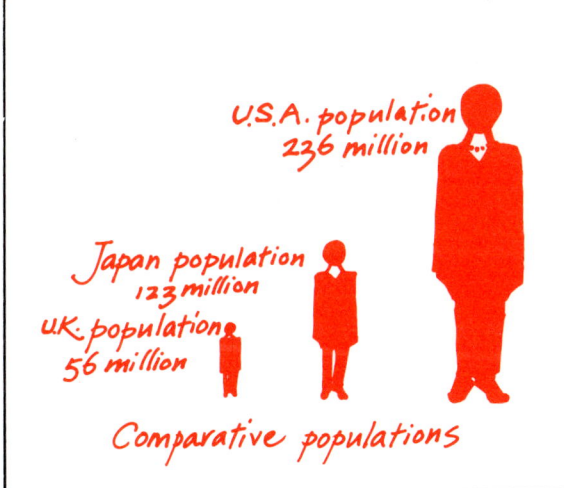

U.S.A. population
236 million

Japan population
123 million

U.K. population
56 million

Comparative populations

Beppu hot spring

Himeji castle

Kyoto Festival

century A.D. there has been very little immigration into Japan. The result was that the Chinese/Korean and South Pacific groups intermarried and blended into what became a distinctly Japanese people.

It has been suggested that the Ainu - the Japanese who live in northern Japan, and who probably originated from Siberia, were the first settlers in the islands. Nowadays, they are treated by most Japanese rather like Red Indians in North America or like Aborigines in Australia - as a quaint old-fashioned people - at best as a tourist attraction. Employment in Ainu villages is below average. The living conditions of many Ainu are poor. For many Japanese people the Ainu are an embarrassment and they do not really want to talk about them.

The Climate

The weather in Japan varies a great deal because the length of the country stretches so far from north to south. Hokkaidō, for example, has cold winters with heavy snowfalls - winter sports are popular, and Sapporo is the centre of a thriving winter sports industry. The southern Ryūkyū Islands, on the other hand, have a sticky sub-tropical climate.

The annual rainfall in Tōkyō is 158 centimetres of which three-quarters falls during the warmer months from April to October. In Japan, June and July are known as the 'rainy season.' (Annual rainfall in London is about 70 cm. The English Lake District has about the same annual rainfall as Tōkyō. Sydney has 118 cms rainfall per year. Adelaide has just 57 cm.)

August to October is the season when Japan is hit by severe storms called typhoons. Typhoons bring terrible winds and drenching rains. Occasionally they are so fierce that the damage to property is enormous. (A very bad typhoon named Kanagawa struck the island of Honshū in 1958. Almost one thousand people were killed.) In winter, however, the winds are usually cold and dry. In Hokkaidō, the temperatures for four months of the year are usually below freezing. The growing season of this Northern Island is only 140 days. Southern Kyūshū and Southern Shikoku have a growing season of 275 days. In these southern parts of Japan the winters are mild, the summers are hot but the rainfall averages over 300 centimetres a year. Because of this long growing season and plentiful rain, two crops of rice a year can be grown.

127

Ainu in his sacred landscape

¥10,000   ¥5,000

¥1,000   ¥500

¥500   ¥100   ¥50   ¥10   ¥5   ¥1

Sapporo Snow Festival

Tropical Ryukyu islands

Nijubashi Bridge —entrance to the Imperial palace.

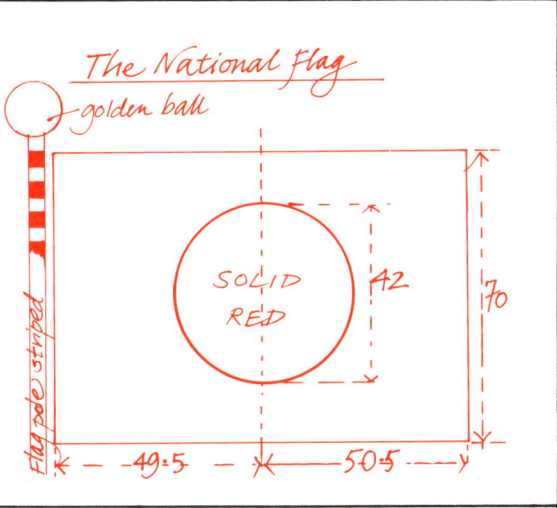

The National Flag

golden ball

SOLID RED

A2

70

Flag pole striped

—49·5—   —50·5—

The Constitution

The Japanese national anthem is called *Kimigayo*. It means 'The Reign of Our Emperor.' It became the national anthem in 1888. Japan has an Imperial family, which is like the royal family in Great Britain.

The Emperor of Japan is no longer directly concerned with the government of his people. This is done by the House of Representatives and the House of Councillors. All people over 20 years of age can vote in elections to choose members for the parliament which is called the Diet. The main political parties in Japan are the Liberal Democratic Party (this has been the ruling party 'in power' since 1956), the Japan Socialist Party, Komeitō, the Democratic Socialist Party and the Japan Communist Party. Japan has a Prime Minister and cabinet ministers like the British system.

Japan is divided into 47 prefectures to help local government (just as England is divided into 43 counties.) Each prefecture has its own local assembly whose members are elected by voters in the community.

Money

Japan's money is based on the Yen. The number of yen to the pound or the dollar varies from day to day but the latest exchange rate can be obtained from travel agents, banks or newspapers.

The Flag

The flag of Japan is a solid red circle on a white background. It is called *Hi no Maru* which means the 'roundness of the sun.' Although this symbol has been popular in Japan since the thirteenth century, it was not adopted as the national flag until 1870.

Defence

Japan has no army but it does have self-defence forces for land, sea and air. It has an agreement with the United States of America about defence.

TO COPY IN YOUR TOPIC BOOK

(filling in the blank spaces)

1. Japan is made up of 4 main........... They are called..........., ..., ... and...........
2. Japan's neighbours are.........., ... and..........
3. The largest island of Japan is called...........
4. About 85% of Japan is..........and this is mostly covered in...........
5. Japan's most famous mountain is...........

TO INVESTIGATE AND REPORT

Imagine you are preparing a journey to Japan. Which route would you choose? Why would you make this choice? How much do you think your return ticket would cost? If you contact a travel agent you can find the answer to this question and any other problems you might have about planning your journey. Use a world map - or, better still, a globe to plot your journey.

TO WRITE ABOUT

Why do you think that the roads of Japan are likely to be much more crowded than our roads?

TO DISCUSS

Most Americans do not refer to Red Indians as First Americans. Most Australians do not talk about Aborigines as First Australians. Few Japanese refer to the Ainu as the First Japanese. Do you think that if a change of names was adopted it would help these groups to be treated with more respect? Do you think that treating these minority groups as quaint tourist attractions harms them in any way? In the U.S.A. some Red Indian chiefs earn a living by posing for photographs with American tourists. In Japan the Ainu are treated in the same way. Do you think it matters?

TO INVESTIGATE AND REPORT

Write a report on the typical weather of your region over the year. Try to include average temperature and rainfall figures. A good atlas should give you the statistics that you need; also, you could contact your local radio station about its weather reports.

Brainstorm Japan

Do you remember the Brainstorm Japan sheets you made in groups at the start of the project? You might think about doing the exercise again in the same groups. But even if you do not repeat the exercise, you should get out your original Brainstorm Japan sheets and read them through once more. Now is the time to discuss your original ideas properly. Why do you think you said these things? Is there anything you would like to change? Is there anything that is wrong? Is there anything you wish you had not said?

Meet together in your original group and discuss your first ideas about Japan. When you have had a good talk about those first thoughts - report back to the whole class. What have you learned about your first impressions. Is it always good to make judgements before you have found out?

A Note For Teachers

Dear Kumiko - Dear John is a Social Studies project for Top Junior and Lower Secondary Schools.

The project was originally written while the author was Headteacher of Hatfield First and Middle School, Sheffield, England. The materials have been well trialled in a number of schools and have been warmly received by pupils and teachers.

An unusual feature of this Japan-focused project is the use of real letters written to pupils in Sheffield Schools from Japanese children in Minami Junior High School, Hiroshima, Sakae Elementary School, Aomori and Funabashi Junior High School, Tōkyō.

Dear Kumiko - Dear John is a general studies project. It is not just a project about Japan. Although it has Japan at its centre, it does not aim to give a comprehensive picture of Japan and the Japanese way of life. Instead, the materials present pictures and impressions in the form of information sheets or letters. It is the author's hope that by the end of the project these will come together in the pupils' minds as empathy for another culture and way of life. It is also hoped that the project materials will lead to increased self-awareness and to a critical investigation of some aspects of the child's own culture.

It is assumed that the children will make full use of other reference books and materials to supplement the resources offered in the text. Some information will only be obtained by contacting local travel agents and estate agents etc.

Dear Kumiko - Dear John is written in the form of a pupils' book. All the materials are presented directly to the pupil. However, the author is fully aware that without the guidance and help of the teacher, much of the work will be superficial and meaningless. This is not a text that assumes the pupils will be self-sufficient and left to get on independently, with work being handed in for marking from time to time.

Many of the materials use a 'World Studies' approach to learning across the curriculum. This means that much of the work is concerned with the needs, values and issues relevant to living in the modern world. It is an approach to learning that has always proved itself in schools throughout the U.K., in Australia and in the U.S.A.

The text makes reference to the Pupils' Project Book. This could take many forms. It might be a loose-leaf folder with different subject sections. It might be an exercise book or a card wallet. The pupil should be encouraged to have some way of keeping the work together so that it can be presented at the end of the project. Some of the work will not be suitable for keeping in this way - it might take the form of a drama or radio play. The pupils might also be encouraged to keep a diary of the work that they have done on the project.

The opportunities offered for class and group discussion are a very important aspect of the work, and are included because the author believes that children must be encouraged to think and talk critically about their world. Children have to be taught these discussion and listening skills - if they are not given the opportunities for this sort of work they have no way of developing the expertise they need.

Discussion Techniques

Getting young people to 'open up' and usefully express their ideas, their opinions and criticisms, their hopes and fears, in group discussion can present the teacher with a formidable challenge. It is easy to be swamped with over-enthusiastic, formless argument. Alternatively, our well-planned, sure-fire stimulus can result in dead silence. Frustratingly, both responses may come at different times from the same class.

The following procedures may help to give shape to attempted discussion sessions, and may help to avoid some of the pitfalls which can occur.

Constructive discussion is more likely when:-

1. As far as possible the teacher plays the part of facilitator rather than leader.
2. All members of the group have equal status.
3. It is a regular part of the classroom practice.
4. Risk and fear is eliminated.
5. There are rules which everyone understands.
6. Good listening is encouraged.

Consider:-

1. The seating arrangements. Can everyone see everyone else? Are you, the teacher, the focal point of the group, or are you seated so as to be a member of it?
2. When children speak do you try to affirm their viewpoint? 'That's a very interesting idea isn't it?'
3. Do you gently try to 'unpack' their jargon - to get beneath their clichés? 'I'm not sure what you mean ...... could you explain a little.'
4. Who raises the questions? Do the children get the chance?
5. Is the group made uncomfortable by silence? Is the teacher afraid of it?
6. When asking a question - does your tone imply the answer you want or expect?
7. In discussion sessions do your questions put pressure on individuals? 'What do you think that means, John? You ought to know the answer to that,' or do you ease the pressure: 'Can anyone think what that means?' 'Have we missed anything here?'
8. The size of the group. Is the group an appropriate size for the sort of discussion you are hoping for? Some activities need fairly small groups of 6 or 7. Brainstorming usually works best in groups this size. Other activities will work if necessary in whole class groups.

Some Activities to Encourage Confidence:-

1. Brainstorming. In small groups members call out ideas on a theme - all of which are recorded by a scribe without comment. No discussion of relevance etc. takes place and the group is encouraged to think as widely as possible. Afterwards the ideas may be more closely considered.
2. Pass an object around the group. Members can only speak when they hold the object. Each member takes a turn but is free to pass the object on without comment. For example the teacher might ask the group to discuss their feelings about Christmas. The object could be a smooth stone. The first person with the 'talking stone' might say 'I look forward to Christmas - because I enjoy getting lots of presents' and then pass the stone to the next person. The next person then makes a comment and passes on the 'talking stone.' Someone who has no comment to make - just passes the stone on to the next person. This activity can help the sort of class where everyone likes to shout out at the same time.
3. Give opening lines for members of the discussion group to

complete. Every member tries to complete the sentence, e.g. at the end of a session offer one of the following:-

I enjoyed the session because................
Today I learned that................
I was surprised when................
It made me angry when................
It was funny when................
If we did it again I would like to................
I didn't think................

Again there is a 'pass' option for those that do not want to comment.

4. Interviews. One member of the group volunteers to be interviewed by the other members of the group. Each member is allowed to ask the interviewee one question. 'If you could be a fly on the wall - on whose wall would you like to be a fly and why?' 'If you could travel anywhere in the world - where would you like to go and why?' Again the interviewee has the right to pass - to decline to answer a question. This activity improves with practice.

5. Word Games. There are many available. Many derive from scouts, cubs and guides. Games like Minister's Cat, Chinese Whispers etc. can all help to build confidence.

Index